WALKS ON DARTMOOR PATHS AND TRACKWAYS

WALKS ON DARTMOOR PATHS AND TRACKWAYS

Michael Caton

Copyright © 2018 Michael Caton
Reprinted 2021

The moral right of the author has been asserted.

Apart from any fair dealing for the purposes of research or private study, or criticism or review, as permitted under the Copyright, Designs and Patents Act 1988, this publication may only be reproduced, stored or transmitted, in any form or by any means, with the prior permission in writing of the publishers, or in the case of reprographic reproduction in accordance with the terms of licences issued by the Copyright Licensing Agency. Enquiries concerning reproduction outside those terms should be sent to the publishers.

Matador
9 Priory Business Park,
Wistow Road, Kibworth Beauchamp,
Leicestershire. LE8 0RX
Tel: 0116 279 2299
Email: books@troubador.co.uk
Web: www.troubador.co.uk/matador
Twitter: @matadorbooks

ISBN 9781788038836

British Library Cataloguing in Publication Data.
A catalogue record for this book is available from the British Library.

Printed and bound by CPI Group (UK) Ltd, Croydon, CR0 4YY
Typeset in 11pt Minion Pro by Troubador Publishing Ltd, Leicester, UK

Matador is an imprint of Troubador Publishing Ltd

To my son Peter who I wish to thank for helping me with the book in many ways including undertaking and commenting on the majority of the walks as well as taking over half of the photographs.

Contents

Acknowledgements	viii
Introduction	ix
The Tracks: origin and history	1
What to see on the walks	5
Advice to walkers	15
The Walks	21
Bibliography	147
Appendix 1 Tracks listed by Crossing and Hemery	149
Appendix 2 Some other useful paths incorporated in the walks	150

Acknowledgements

I wish to thank the following who have also checked out walks: Anne and Roger MacDonald, Rob and Rose Gillingham, David Martin, Val Barnes and my son David and his family. I am further indebted to Bill Radcliffe who has accompanied me on several of the walks and provided much valuable information from his extensive Dartmoor knowledge.

I thank my wife Margaret who has been my companion on numerous Dartmoor walks over the years.

Finally I thank Margaret and Peter for checking the proofs.

Introduction

I first walked on Dartmoor in the 1950s and in the years that have elapsed since then have been privileged to visit there many times in all seasons and weathers. It is my hope that in writing this book I may pass on to others some of the pleasure I have experienced in this very special place.

What is it about Dartmoor that is so appealing? To me it is a combination of its wild unspoilt character, magnificent scenery and the numerous prehistoric and historic remains. Whereas much of the southern part of England is either built on or in use as agricultural land, Dartmoor stands out as a large area of wild open moorland where the visitor can wander at will and forget the noise, artefacts and bustle of the modern world. Its size and dimensions are such that in the centre of the remotest parts it is possible to be four or five miles from the nearest public road and experience the feeling of remoteness, sense of adventure and challenge of exploring an extensive area of wild country with map and compass.

It is an area of fine scenery. Some of this is to be found in the valleys where the rivers, which rise on the high moor, often pass over mini cascades or larger waterfalls and through fine gorges such as the Dart Valley below Dartmeet and Tavy Cleave. The tors, outcrops of granite of various shapes and sizes on many of the moorland heights, are another attractive feature of the moor and those who climb them find that they provide fine viewpoints, often for many miles around. Then there is the colour of the moorland as it changes with the seasons from brown in winter to green in spring and summer and the purple of the heather in August. Even the remotest parts of the moor can be very colourful; I have visited the wild area above East Dart Head in the height of summer when it was ablaze with the yellow of the Bog Asphodel and the white Cotton Grass.

I owe my introduction to Dartmoor to a lady, Marjory Eckett Fielden, who lived next door to my family in Torquay in the 1950s. It was Mrs Fielden who, when I was at home for my university vacations, encouraged me to visit the moor. She had known Dartmoor for many years and had a knowledge and love of it she was able to convey to me which led to my own lifetime fascination.

Over the years I have undertaken many walks alone, with my family and with members of the Dartmoor Preservation Association (DPA), notably with the Association's London Group where I have been privileged to lead walks on many visits to the moor. In planning the walks in this book I have tried to address the needs of those who wish to venture well into the open moor, as well as shorter walks, over routes which are relatively easy to negotiate and as far as possible avoid passing through rough and miry ground.

This led me to seek out suitable paths and trackways and in recent years I have worked out a series of walks, some of which form the subject of this book. Over half of these take a circular course but in other cases the return is by the same route as a round course would be difficult to achieve without much road walking, climbing or negotiating rough ground. There are inevitably a few sections where paths do not exist and here I have endeavoured to describe routes over open moor which are easy to follow.

The routes described of course cover only a fraction of the huge range of possible walks that can be taken on Dartmoor but they have been selected to represent as much of the moor as possible. They are of varying length with a few very short walks of around 2–3 miles with a maximum of 7½ miles. The central area of the northern wilderness, where there are few tracks and longer distances would be involved, has not been included.

Some of the paths are well known and are shown on the maps whereas others, as far as I am aware, have not been recorded. In all cases I have followed the routes, if necessary establishing the best ways by trial and error. In recent years I have made extensive use of Google Earth in checking their position. This a most valuable tool since it shows up all but the narrowest paths and is recommended to anyone planning walks. It also shows at a glance how some areas, such as Holne Moor, are crossed by a complex system of paths whereas in other areas they are relatively sparse.

I must stress that this is wild Dartmoor and the paths and tracks are not laid out as if they are in a municipal public park! They can be rough and uneven but for most of their length provide reasonable walking for those who are suitably equipped.

The mileages, as measured on the OS Explorer 1:25 000 scale map are minimum distances since walking on the moor often takes ins and outs which deviate from the route traced on the map. I have not included walking times as these vary considerably with individual walking speeds but would advise allowing considerably more time than for similar distances along a tarmac road. Paces are included in some of the descriptions to give an approximate guide to distances between key points. Pace lengths obviously vary with the individual so this can only be a rough guide.

The walks have been arranged for convenience in a sequence, starting from the Widecombe area, around the southern moor, that is the areas of moor south of the Tavistock to Moretonhampstead road, and in a similar way round the northern moor.

In writing up the walks I have generally used the word "path" to describe ways of footpath ie pedestrian width, whereas the term "track" has been reserved for those wide enough to take carts, although these are mostly not suitable or open for motor vehicle use. There is, however, a considerable grey area between these and the words are to some extent interchangeable. In the introductory sections, for simplicity, I have generally referred to them all as tracks.

I have included here sections briefly describing the origin and history of the tracks and accounts of the many interesting features of the moor to be seen on the walks, referring the reader interested in further details to the numerous publications on these subjects.

A selection of photographs, placed in the central pages of the book, illustrate some of the places and features seen on the walks.

Michael Caton
Photo by my Grandaughter Ruth Foulsham.

The Tracks: Origin and History

When writing this book I have made extensive use of the *Ordnance Survey Dartmoor Explorer Map* and the *British Mountain Map* and I advise readers to obtain copies of these before following the text.

Most of the walks use sections of several tracks which are of many different origins and age. Some of them are ancient routes which have served such purposes as access to the moor for peat cutting, farming and mining, as transmoor packhorse routes for conveying fleece and yarn by wool-jobbers and possibly for monks travelling between Buckfast, Buckland and Tavistock abbeys. Two classic works have described these routes: *Guide to Dartmoor* by William Crossing and *Walking Dartmoor's Ancient Tracks* by Eric Hemery. Crossing's list of tracks is by far the longer whereas Hemery described a smaller number in more detail. I have not always been able to locate the exact alignments from Crossing and Hemery's instructions and in all cases have retraced the routes and described the tracks I have been able to find on the ground. However there is no way of knowing that the routes correspond to the precise course followed by the original users. A list of tracks from these two sources with cross references is shown in Appendix 1.

In some cases paths that run along the course of leats are used. These are artificial channels cut through the moorland on gently falling gradients to convey water from intake points on the rivers to supply farms, mines, industry, corn mills or for domestic use. Some of them can be seen running round the hillsides for many miles. The majority are now disused and paths run beside or along the floor of their former channel. With those still in use paths alongside them are followed. Two books *Follow the Leat* by John Robbins and *Walking The Dartmoor Waterways* by Eric Hemery are useful sources of reference on leats.

The trackbed of former railways and tramways are also incorporated into some of the walks, notably the Zeal Tor Tramroad from Shipley Bridge, South Brent, to Western Whittabarrow; the Redlake China Clay tramway near Ivybridge and the Rattlebrook peat railway near Lydford. These have a firm surface and afford easy routes well into the moor. Details of them are available in *Walking The Dartmoor Railroads* by Eric Hemery.

Other tracks, some of which are shown on the maps, may have been created by walkers or are of unknown origin, at least to me. A list of the more significant of these is shown in Appendix 2.

Abbot's Way / Jobber's Road

The Abbot's Way, which features in several of the walks, and is probably the best known of Dartmoor's tracks, requires special mention and some explanation. It has been claimed that this formed a link between the abbeys of Buckfast to the south of the moor and Buckland and Tavistock on the west, although it would of course have ceased to be used for this purpose after the dissolution of the monasteries in the 1530s. However there has been controversy, notably by Worth and Hemery, over its origin and use as a route by the monks. In fact it was first mentioned in print by a traveller named Andrews in 1794, over two hundred years after the dissolution.

Hemery used the name Jobber's Road for it on the grounds of its use as a trans moorland route by the wool jobbers for fleece and yarn collecting and cloth delivery journeys in connection with the woollen industry of Buckfastleigh. Crossing also noted that on the moor this old way is usually known as Jobber's Path. However the name Abbot's Way has long been adopted by the Ordnance Survey and is also used by the British Mountain Map for the eastern part of the route. This name is generally understood by moorland walkers. I have therefore used it here; after all even if it is misleading, what is wrong with a name with an air of mystery and romance which has been in use for over two hundred years?

The track enters the moor at Cross Furzes (700666) 2½ miles west of Buckfast Abbey and follows a course via the Avon and Erme valleys to an inscribed boundary stone above Erme Head known as Broad Rock (618672).

At Broad Rock the track divides and there is a difference of opinion over the origin of the two branches. Crossing claimed that a branch to the left led via Plym Steps (603672) and the Sheepstor area to Buckland Abbey, whereas the other, which is named Abbot's Way by the OS and shown running north west across the high ground to Plym Ford (611684), led via Nuns Cross (602699) and the area where Princetown now stands to Tavistock.

However Hemery claimed that the two tracks diverged at Plym Steps, the Tavistock branch then ascending and running west of Lower Harter Tor, then across the Eylesbarrow Mine Track and on to Nuns Cross where it came together with the Crossing route.

Hemery says the route across the high ground from Broad Rock to Plym Ford is an old peat track. However no track appears to exist in the alignment shown by the OS whereas a clear track, which has become a broadway in recent years and is very useful to walkers, crosses this section along a course further to the east as I have described in walk 14. Part of this route is shown on the British Mountain Map. The continuation of this northward is shown on the maps by a route which runs diagonally to the right and then round a right angle bend to the left leading to Nun's Cross. I have been unable to find the central part of this section and doubt its usefulness as a through route for walkers.

There are paths along much of the way on the section from Broad Rock to Plym Steps, notably onwards from where it crossed the Deadman's Bottom Stream, but the upper portion is more problematic and I am unable to recommend a continuous route throughout.

What to see on the walks

There is much to see on Dartmoor, both natural features and relics of human activity from prehistoric to modern times. Below are brief details of the main features seen on the walks with reference to the extensive literature on these subjects.

Tors

The granite outcrops on many of the hills known as tors are perhaps the best known feature of the Dartmoor landscape. Dartmoor is a granite upland and the tors are the hard rocks remaining after centuries of weathering. A number of them have been worn into curious shapes and they are fascinating to explore as well as being fine view points. Some have depressions in the rocks known as rock basins. These are formed by weathering brought about by trapped water, frost and wind.

Rocks have often moved down from the tors and deposited on the hillsides during the process of weathering. These, known as clitter, cover considerable areas.

Prehistoric Remains

The very extensive prehistoric monuments, mainly of the Bronze Age, are an outstanding feature of Dartmoor and their exploration is a subject of endless fascination. The durability of the readily available granite, used for their construction and the remoteness of Dartmoor has ensured their survival over some 3,000 years. Remains of homesteads, field systems, burial and ritual monuments are to be found on most parts of the moor. Below are brief accounts of these: for further details the reader is referred to books on the subject including *Worth's Dartmoor, Prehistoric Dartmoor* by Paul Pettit and *Dartmoor Atlas of Antiquities* by Jeremy Butler which includes detailed descriptions of the sites with associated maps.

Hut Circles and Pounds

Hut circles or round houses, of which there are several thousand on the moor, are the ruined walls of dwellings. They occur singly but more often in groups, the latter in many cases being surrounded by a walled enclosure known as a pound. The walls of the huts would have stood about four feet high, the roof being of wooden material and turf. Some of the huts are thought to have been used as cattle pens or for storage. Upright stones which formed the door jambs at the hut entrances are often evident and excavation has revealed cooking holes and postholes indicating the position of the wooden roof supports. Stone platforms are found in some huts which may have been for sleeping purposes.

Reaves

Reaves are prehistoric field boundaries, consisting of low banks of earth and small stones. They form an extensive system across many parts of the moor and indicate how the various sites of occupation were interconnected. Some of them form a useful guide for the walker and sections of the walks have reaves running alongside them. For further information on this subject the reader is referred to *The Dartmoor Reaves* by Andrew Fleming.

Cairns and Cists

Cairns or barrows are abundant on Dartmoor. They consist of round mounds of stones which were placed over burial sites. Cairns are often surrounded by a stone retaining or cairn circle and many have a central cist. Some of the larger cairns were built on the hilltops where they are prominent features.

Cists, also known as kistvaens, are stone chests used as burial chambers. When complete they have four sides and a cover stone, although some of these parts are often missing. A number of cists have been excavated when flint tools and pottery remains were discovered. Cists vary in size very considerably, an example of a very large one being at Roundy Park (walks 18, 19).

Stone Circles

In addition to the cairn circles referred to above, there are a number of larger circles some of which are not associated with other monuments.

Menhirs and Stone Rows

Menhirs or standing stones are found in many parts of the moor. They vary in height, the tallest, at Drizzlecombe (walks 10, 11) being 14 feet. Stone rows, alignments of upright stones of varying size and length, are a particular feature of Dartmoor where most of those in Britain are to be found. The longest, in the Erme Valley is over 2 miles and the shortest just a few yards. The tallest, on Stalldon, has some stones over 6 feet in height whereas the majority rise no more than 2 feet above the ground. The rows occur singly or in two or three parallel alignments.

The rows are usually found in conjunction with other structures and a typical row has a cairn at one end and a menhir or a flat upright blocking stone at the other. Their use is unknown, although their association with stone circles and burials suggests a religious function and various theories have been put forward on their possible astronomical significance. A few menhirs stand alone.

Monument Complexes

In some parts of the moor the above monuments occur together, with several stone rows, circles, cairns and cists forming complex associations. Notable examples are at Drizzlecombe (walk 10, 11), Merrivale (walk 22) and Shovel Down (walk 28).

Medieval and later human activities

Tinning

Tin extraction took place on Dartmoor from medieval times until the early part of the twentieth century and there are extensive remains of this important industry over many parts of the moor. Much has been written on this subject and books for information include *Worth's Dartmoor and The Dartmoor Tin Industry A Field Guide* by Phil Newman.

Tinning from the twelth to the eighteenth century took place in the valleys where the stream and river beds were scoured for tin ore, leaving extensive earthworks. Heaps of discarded stones and gullies show the extent of excavation carried out in the search for this metal. Among these are to be found the ruins of blowing houses or blowing mills; small rectangular buildings in which the ore was smelted. They contained a furnace and a water wheel to operate bellows to produce a forced draught. Remains of these, including the wheelpits and associated water channels, are to be found in many of these sites as well as mortar stones with one or more circular cavities for crushing the tin ore and mould stones with rectangular depressions for forming ingots from the molten tin. In some places there are caches or beehive huts built by the tinners for shelter or for a place to keep their tools.

More recent tin mining, which reached its peak activity in the nineteenth century and continued into the twentieth, was on a much larger scale and involved mine shafts to reach tin ore at a much deeper level. These operations left behind very extensive earthworks which, together with the remains of associated buildings and leats, are prominent features of their former sites. Some of them, e.g. Eylesbarrow (walks 15, 16), Huntingdon (walks 4, 5) and Whiteworks (walk 16) are noted on the routes described.

Stone Crosses

There are over a hundred granite crosses on Dartmoor and its borders. They date mainly from the medieval period but a few are relatively modern, having been erected in Victorian times or later. They served a variety of purposes but the majority of those on the open moor, encountered in these walks, were probably either set up as boundary stones or as wayside markers in association with trackways, some of the latter having monastic associations. A few crosses, notably Spurrell's (walk 7), Nun's (walks 13, 15) and Horn's (walk 3) mark intersections of tracks. One line of fourteen crosses marks a possible medieval route across the moor, the Maltern Way or Monk's Path (walks 3, 12, 13, 15). Other crosses have been erected in more recent times as memorials.

The crosses are simple in structure but vary considerably in size and shape. Some of them have been re-erected after lying fallen on the ground for many years. In some cases restoration has involved construction of a new shaft to which the original ancient cross head has been attached.

Books by William Crossing, *The Ancient Stone Crosses of Dartmoor*, FH Starkey *Dartmoor Crosses*, Bill Harrison,

Dartmoor Stone Crosses and Tim Sandles', *A Pilgrimage to Dartmoor Crosses* cover this subject in detail and provide accounts of their description and history.

Many of these noble monuments were no doubt an invaluable aid to those negotiating the Dartmoor wilderness in earlier centuries and it is good to know that they are still there to guide walkers in the twenty-first century. In clear weather they can often be seen from a distance, helping to locate the route and when visibility is poor, as they come into view, they can be a welcome sign that the correct course had been followed.

Guide and Boundary Stones

The crosses were way markers of the medieval period. In more recent times simple stones or pillars were used for this purpose usually with inscribed initial letters of the relevant border towns to indicate the direction to these places. Other stones mark boundaries of the Dartmoor Forest[1] and parishes. Like the crosses, these are useful route markers for the walks. *A Field Guide to the Boundary Markers on and Around Dartmoor* by Dave Brewer covers this subject in detail.

Clapper Bridges

Clapper bridges, made of slabs of granite resting on granite piers, are a well-known feature of Dartmoor. They range from one to three spans and vary considerably in size from the large structures such as the famous one over the East Dart at Postbridge to small single spans across streams and leats. The oldest, such as those at Postbridge and Bellever, are medieval in origin, providing crossings for ancient trackways, whereas others were built in modern times for a variety of purposes such as farm access.

Clappers provide valuable links for walkers where river crossing would otherwise be difficult.

---

1 An area of land reserved as a hunting ground for the king.

Rabbit Warrening

Commercial breeding of rabbits took place on Dartmoor until the 1950s when the myxomatosis epidemic wiped out most of the rabbit population. There is much evidence of this activity, known as warrening, on several parts of the moor. Warrens included a house where the warrener lived, two of which – Ditsworthy (walk 10) and Trowlesworthy (walk 9) both in the Plym Valley – are seen on the walks, as well as the sites of others, now ruined. Prominent features of the warrens are the oblong pillow mounds or buries built for the rabbits to burrow in. The remains of vermin traps constructed to capture stoats and weasels which preyed on the rabbits are also to be seen. The rabbits were caught by the warrener, dogs driving them into large nets when they would be killed and sold for their meat and skins.

Farms

Although most Dartmoor farms are located around the moor, a few have been built well into the moorland area and include the warrens which also carried out farming activities. Most of these are now disused but they are an interesting feature of Dartmoor's history and the human struggle to make a living in this wild upland area. A full account of those which lie within the boundary of the Dartmoor Forest is given in *Dartmoor Forest Farms* by Elizabeth Stanbrook.

Newtakes

There are numerous dry stone walls on Dartmoor which surround areas reclaimed from the moor in comparatively recent times. These are known as newtakes.

Flora and Fauna

Although conditions are harsh, there is an interesting range of flowering plants on the open moor which provide colour especially in summer. Best known of these are the heathers of which there are three species: Bell Heather, Cross Leaved Heath and Ling. The Whortleberry (or Bilberry), like heather a small shrub, has edible purple-black fruit in July and August. Other common moorland plants include the Tormentil which has yellow four-petalled flowers, the Milkwort, with a range of colours from pink to blue and the Heath Bedstraw, with white flowers in short clusters. Gorse, both the dwarf variety and the taller Common Gorse, grow extensively and bracken covers considerable areas of the moor.

The white Cotton Grass and yellow Bog Asphodel add colour to wet upland areas and in the valley bogs are to be found the Sundew, an insectivorous plant which catches and digests its prey in rosettes of leaves with red hairs and a number of other interesting plants including yellow Marsh St. John's Wort, the dark blue Lesser Scullcap, Ivy Leaved Bell flower and Marsh Violet.

There are also many rushes and grasses as well as mosses, liverworts and lichens. A particular favourite of mine is the luminous moss (*Schistostega Osmundacea*) which grows in rock and wall crevices as well as in cave-like structures. This emits a greenish-yellow glow as a consequence of absorbing and then re-emitting incoming light. It is quite rare but well worth looking for.

High Dartmoor is largely devoid of trees except for conifer plantations, a feature of modern times and three ancient oak woods: Piles Wood, Wistmans Wood and Black Tor Copse high up the river valleys. The red berries of Mountain Ash bushes are a delightful sight in the autumn.

The ponies are the best known of the animals seen on Dartmoor. These are not wild but, like the cattle and sheep, are owned by farmers who have grazing rights on the moor. Wild mammals include foxes and rabbits as well as badgers, stoats, weasels and mink.

There is a variety of birds including the Skylark, Stonechat, Meadow Pipit, Pied Wagtail, Lapwing, Ring Ouzel, Dipper, Red Grouse, Curlew and Buzzard.

Of the reptiles, lizards and adders are probably the best known.

Advice to Walkers

Using this guide

This book has been written with the serious walker in mind, for those with some experience of walking on Dartmoor or in similar country elsewhere. Dartmoor is a wild place and it is easy to lose the way especially on the longer walks and in misty weather. It is essential to bring and be able to use a map and compass and preferably a GPS. Less experienced walkers are advised to try first the shorter walks which are all near the edge of the moor.

The walk descriptions are accompanied by maps on which the approximate alignment of the routes is indicated by bold black lines. An overview map of Dartmoor shows the starting point of each walk. It is recommended that the routes are planned before setting out and checked on the *Dartmoor OS Explorer* and *Dartmoor British Mountain* maps, also, if possible, on Google Earth. I have used the latter, on which most of the tracks are visible, to check each route and recommend it as a most valuable aid to exploring the moor. The British Mountain Map has a wealth of useful information on the back including visitor information, navigation, code of conduct and emergency procedures.

Grid references have been quoted for key points; these have either been read off the OS 1:25 000 map or located with a GPS especially where the feature referred to does not appear on the map. In most cases six figure references are quoted but in a few cases eight figures are used to give a more precise identification where this might be helpful. In the event of losing a path make for the next reference point or a feature shown on the map.

The golden rule of walking on Dartmoor is always know where you are; don't wander aimlessly. Dartmoor is a large area of wild country and it is easy to get lost.

Whereas I have endeavoured to provide enough instructions to enable the tracks to be located, it is not possible to describe every twist and turn they make or to indicate every branch. Some of them are rather ragged at the edges and short sections may be indistinct or even missing, in which case it is necessary to take care that the continuation is correctly followed.

I must emphasise that although the majority of the tracks have remained largely unchanged for many years, changes do occur from time to time and I therefore cannot guarantee that they have all remained exactly as described in the text.

With those walks that return by the same route it is important on the outward walk to note features that may help to identify the course on the return.

River banks are referred to in the text as left or right by the usual convention ie as if facing downstream, regardless of the direction of walking.

Transport

Each walk starts at a suitable parking place, although in some cases space for vehicles is very limited and it may be necessary to park further away. Public transport is generally sparse around and across the moor except along the west and south borders. Regrettably some bus routes are very infrequent and it may not be possible to arrange walks to fit in with their schedules. Most walks start a considerable distance from the bus stop and thus require significant road walking which adds extra mileage to the walk. Bus timetables are liable to change and it is not appropriate to give specific timetable details here. Current timetable information can be obtained by contacting Traveline 08712002233, the national park visitor centres (see p 20) and local timetables.

Rail services are available at Ivybridge on the south of the moor and on summer Sundays at Okehampton in the north.

The use of taxis may be considered to avoid long and tiring road walks.

Military Firing

Extensive areas of northern Dartmoor are used for live firing by the military and the public is excluded when this is taking place. There are three firing areas – Okehampton, Willsworthy and Merrivale – the boundaries of which are marked on the OS and British Mountain Maps and on leaflets available from the National Park. However only three of the walks, (23, 26 and 27), enter the ranges although some others run close to them. This is noted in these three walk descriptions and it is essential to check whether firing is taking place before setting out.

The boundaries of each firing area are marked on the moor with red and white poles and warning signals, red flags by day and red lamps at night, are displayed on prominent physical features in the area. Details of firing times are published in advance in local newspapers on the preceding Friday or can be obtained by dialing Freephone 0800 4584868. Updated daily information on the firing is broadcast every morning on BBC Radio Devon. Also the firing programme six weeks in advance can be obtained at www.gov.uk/government/publications/dartmoor-firing-programme. There are certain guaranteed non live firing times including the month of August.

Do not touch any military debris which may be unexploded ammunition and very dangerous. If a suspicious object is seen note the position and inform the military authorities (01837 657210) or the police (999).

The Weather

Dartmoor is an upland area and has a high rainfall. There are also strong winds and mists. It is thus necessary to be prepared for these as well as frosts and snow in winter. It is important to check the local weather forecast before going ahead with the walks.

When walking in mists it is essential to be able to navigate with a compass and preferably a GPS. Mists can arise quite suddenly so be prepared.

I do not advise walking on the moor when there is a significant amount of snow on the ground as it can obscure the tracks as well as holes and uneven ground features which may be dangerous to walk over.

Crossing Rivers and Streams

I have tried to avoid stream and river crossings when planning the walks but in many cases this is not possible if a reasonable amount of Dartmoor is to be included. The crossing points included should present no major difficulty except after heavy or prolonged rain when they can rapidly swell in volume, turn into rushing torrents and become impossible or dangerous to cross. As a general rule only cross when able to do so comfortably.

What to Wear

Walking on Dartmoor, as in any upland area, requires suitable clothing. Footwear needs to be strong and robust and walking boots are recommended. Waterproofs must, of course be taken even if the weather is fine at the outset as conditions can change in the course of the day. Wear sufficient to keep warm and take extra layers of clothing to be prepared if the temperature falls. Some form of headgear is also very important to prevent heat loss in winter and provide protection from the sun in summer. Tics which carry Lyme disease can be a problem on the moor, so avoid contact with these by keeping the skin covered, wearing long socks and trousers.

Food and Drink

Always take plenty to eat and drink. In hot weather particularly it is easy to become dehydrated.

Safety, in case of emergency

Always carry a first aid kit and medical supplies. Also take a mobile phone, although there is not always network coverage on parts of the moor. Leave details of your route with someone before setting out. If help is required phone 999 and ask for Dartmoor Rescue.

Further information on moorland safety matters can be obtained at the Dartmoor National Park website:

www.dartmoor.gov.uk

It should be said that it is the walker's responsibility to make sure they are able to undertake the walks and that they do so at their own risk.

Dartmoor a National Park

Dartmoor has been a National Park since 1951. This means that its natural beauty, wildlife and cultural heritage are protected, although sadly over the years the moor has been threatened in many ways including the planting of conifers on the open moorland, reservoir schemes and china clay extraction.

However the moor has not changed significantly since I first knew it in the 1950s and it remains a large area of wild country of national importance.

The National Park Authority has three visitor centres. The principal one of these, the High Moorland Centre, is at Princetown 01822 890414, with others (summer only) at Postbridge 01822 880272 and Haytor 01364 661520. These have available a wide variety of valuable information about the moor and all walkers are recommended to call there.

The Walks

1	Top, Pil and Tunhill
2	Along Hamel Down to Grimspound
3	Ryders Hill
4	Huntingdon Warren and Broadafalls
5	Abbot's Way to the Avon Valley
6	Western Whittabarrow
7	Three Barrows
8	Piles Copse
9	Trowlesworthy Bronze Age Remains
10	Ditsworthy Warren and Drizzlecombe
11	The Langcombe Valley and Grim's Grave
12	Nun's Cross from Burrator Lake
13	Black Tor Falls and Crazy Well Pool
14	Upper Plym Valley and Erme Head
15	Fox Tor and Childe's Tomb
16	Whiteworks to Duck's Pool
17	Bellever Tor from Dunnabridge Pound
18	Along the East Dart from Postbridge
19	Waterfall, East Dart
20	Brown's House, West Dart
21	Devonport Leat and Wistman's Wood
22	Great Mis Tor and Merrivale
23	The Walkham Valley
24	Upper Rattlebrook Valley
25	Black Tor, West Okement Valley
26	Yes Tor and High Willhays
27	Steeperton Gorge
28	Teignhead Farm

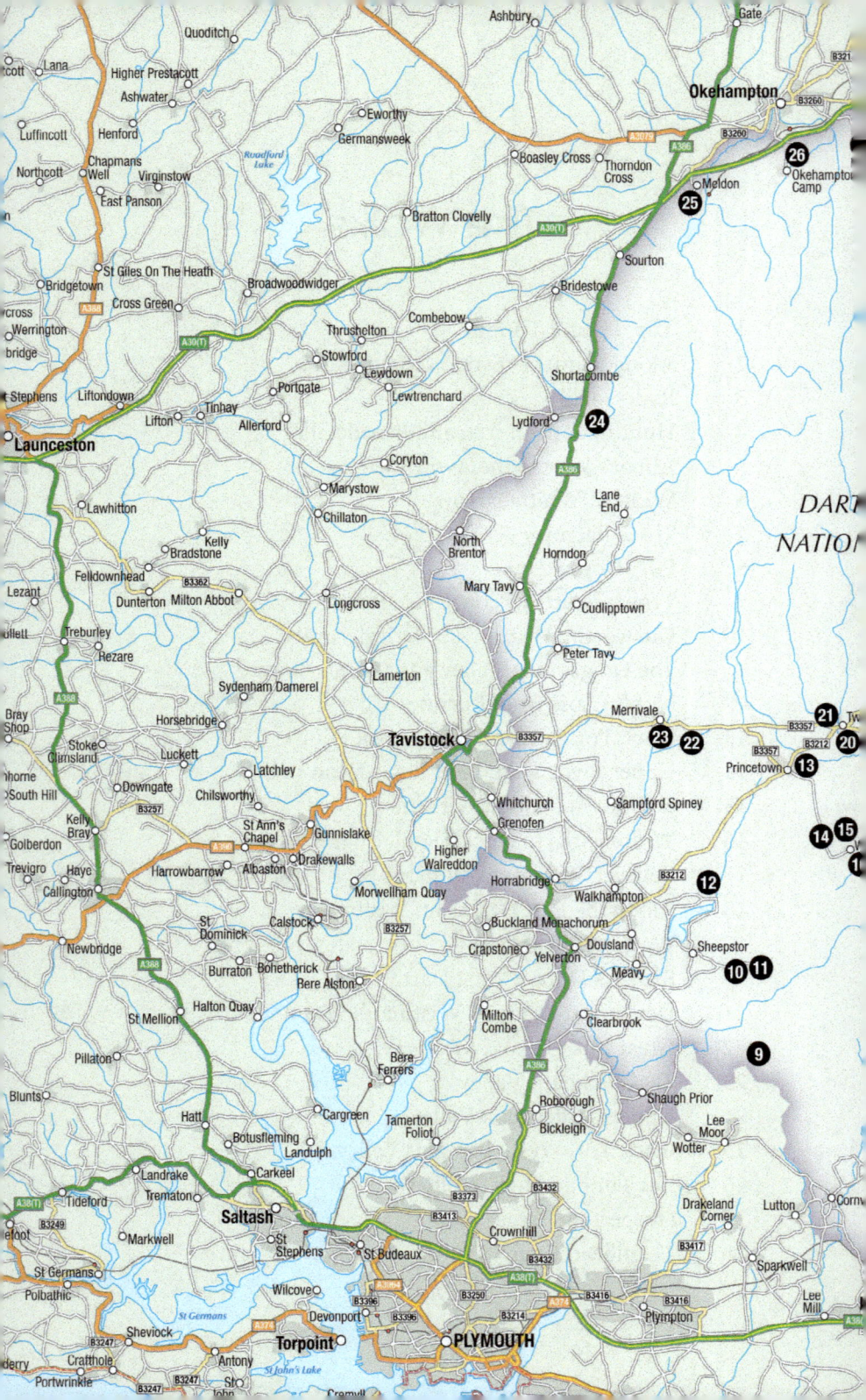

1

Top, Pil and Tunhill – *2 miles*

This first walk is a short circular route from near the top of Widecombe Hill. It is easy going with fine views and is a good introduction to Dartmoor.

Start
Car park (735768) on the left of the road from Widecombe to Haytor road near Harefoot Cross.

From the car park cross the road and follow the track to Top Tor (736762). Pass between the rocks of the tor and continue along the track which runs diagonally to the right leading to Pil Tor (735760). The way again passes between the rocks and bends right to lead on to Tunhill Rocks (732758).

There are views from the route to the right, west across the Widecombe valley to the ridge of Hamel Down and Haytor, Saddle and Rippon Tors are to the left. The hill ahead to the south is Wittaburrow.

A small prehistoric enclosure is seen on the approach to Tunhill Rocks, surrounding two hut circles.

The route continues along a path which runs south from the approach to the rocks through bracken and gorse to join an old track known as the Tunhill Road (733755).This runs from the road below Rippon Tor to Blackslade and Tunhill in the Widecombe Valley. Turn left along this and walk for twenty paces to a point where the track bends to the right. Here a short

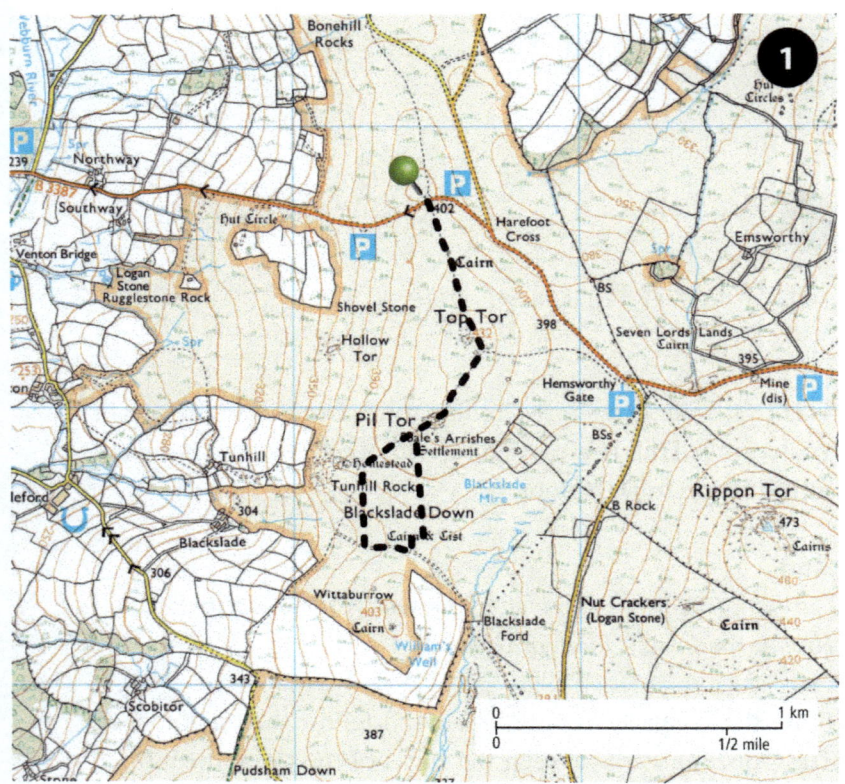

distance to the left is a fine cist (734755). This is on a low mound and has all four sides in position.

For the return walk follow a path which runs past the east side of the cist and leads back to Pil Tor. Walk up to the tor and then pass to the left of it to join the outward route which is retraced back to the start.

A small deviation can be made to visit Foales Arishes, an interesting complex of reaves in which are built hut circles. This lies on the hillside to the east of the route.

2

Along Hamel Down to Grimspound – 5½ miles

Another recommended walk in the Widecombe area follows the high ridge of Hamel Down to the Bronze Age settlement of Grimspound. This is longer than walk 1 with some climbing but there are good paths and splendid views.

Start

Car park by the summit of Southcombe Lane (708764) west of Widecombe

Follow the broad green way which branches, north, from the car park. After ½ mile the track meets a stone wall.

The route now follows the course of the Two Moors Way, a long-distance footpath from Ivybridge, south of Dartmoor, to Lynton in North Devon. The way continues alongside the wall for a few hundred yards and then ascends the ridge to Hameldown Beacon. On the right of the track there is a cist (710783) which has three sides partly covered by a capstone.

Hameldown Beacon is capped by a prehistoric barrow. The stone upper wall of a newtake on the west side of the ridge passes over the summit. There is an inscribed boundary stone, bearing the name Broad Burrow, on the beacon, one of several on the ridge. These were set up by the Duke of Somerset in 1854 to mark the boundary of his lands of Natsworthy Manor.

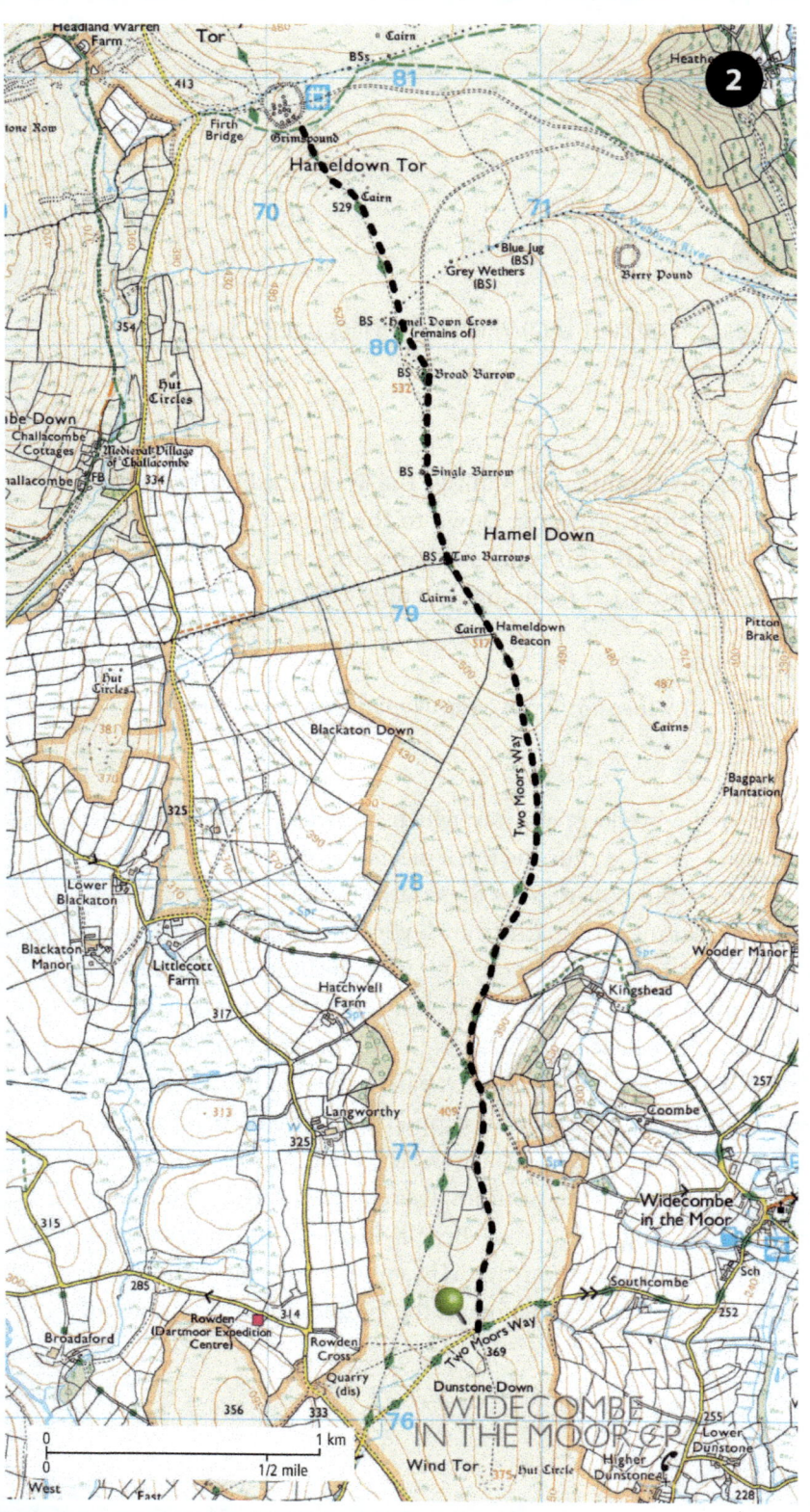

The scenery here is magnificent with views of Haytor and the surrounding tors to the south east, right, and a wide area of central Dartmoor to the left. Looking back, to the south, is a panorama of much of the South Devon coast.

Continue, with the wall on the left, to Two Barrows (707792) where the wall bends sharply left downhill. The track is seen ahead as it continues along the ridge to Broad Barrow (706799), a much larger structure than those previously seen. The small Single Barrow is seen on the left about half way along this section of the route. On approaching Broad Barrow there is a path, branching to the left, bypassing that point which can be followed as an alternative. Avoid a track which branches to the right from here.

The track is then followed to Hameldown Tor (703806), passing Hameldown Cross (704801), seen a short distance away on the left. This is a very roughly shaped specimen, with one arm and part of the top missing. It carries the inscription HC DS 1854 reflecting its use, like the boundary stones, as a marker of the lands of Natsworthy Manor. It was erected here in 1854, the letters DS being the initials of the Duke of Somerset.

Beyond Hameldown Tor the way descends north west to Grimspound (701809). This well-known Bronze Age settlement with enclosure wall and 24 hut circles is an impressive sight and I well remember the excitement of seeing it for the first time on one of my early Dartmoor walks in the 1950s. There is an imposing entrance to the pound and to descend to this and pass through it into the enclosure is an experience of a bygone age leaving one wondering what it was like when our Bronze Age ancestors lived here all those years ago.

It was excavated by the Dartmoor Exploration Committee in the 1890s and considerable restoration took place. The walls of a hut near the centre were reconstructed to their original height. There is an entrance passage and two jamb stones are placed either side of the entrance. A stream, the Grimslake, runs through the pound.

Beyond Grimspound is Hookney Tor. A fine cist, marked 'cairn' on the OS map lies 500 yards north east of the pound (704812) and can be reached by following a track which passes west–east through the pound to where it forks and then striking northwards across the moor.

The same route is recommended for the return walk.

3

Ryders Hill – 5 ½ miles

Ryders Hill, a fine viewpoint on the southern moor, can be approached across Holne Moor from the Holne to Hexworthy road.

Start
Combestone Tor Car Park (670718)

There are numerous paths and tracks on Holne Moor which can be very confusing to the walker. Many of these arose from the nineteenth century mining activities in that area but two of them – the Combestone or Cumston Road and Sandy Way – are ancient and are followed for most of the walk.

The first section is along the Cumston Road. This is a direct route from Hexworthy to South Brent and would have been used by the moorland farming communities travelling to the South Brent market and fair. It runs initially in a southerly direction to Horn's Cross. To enter it cross the road from the tor and follow the path which branches from the road opposite the left hand, east, side of the car park. This is not very obvious at first but it becomes clearer as it ascends the hill. The general direction to take is towards the mid point of the left slope of the low hill which lies immediately ahead.

Take care to avoid entering a more prominent path which branches from the road to the right of the Cumston Road.

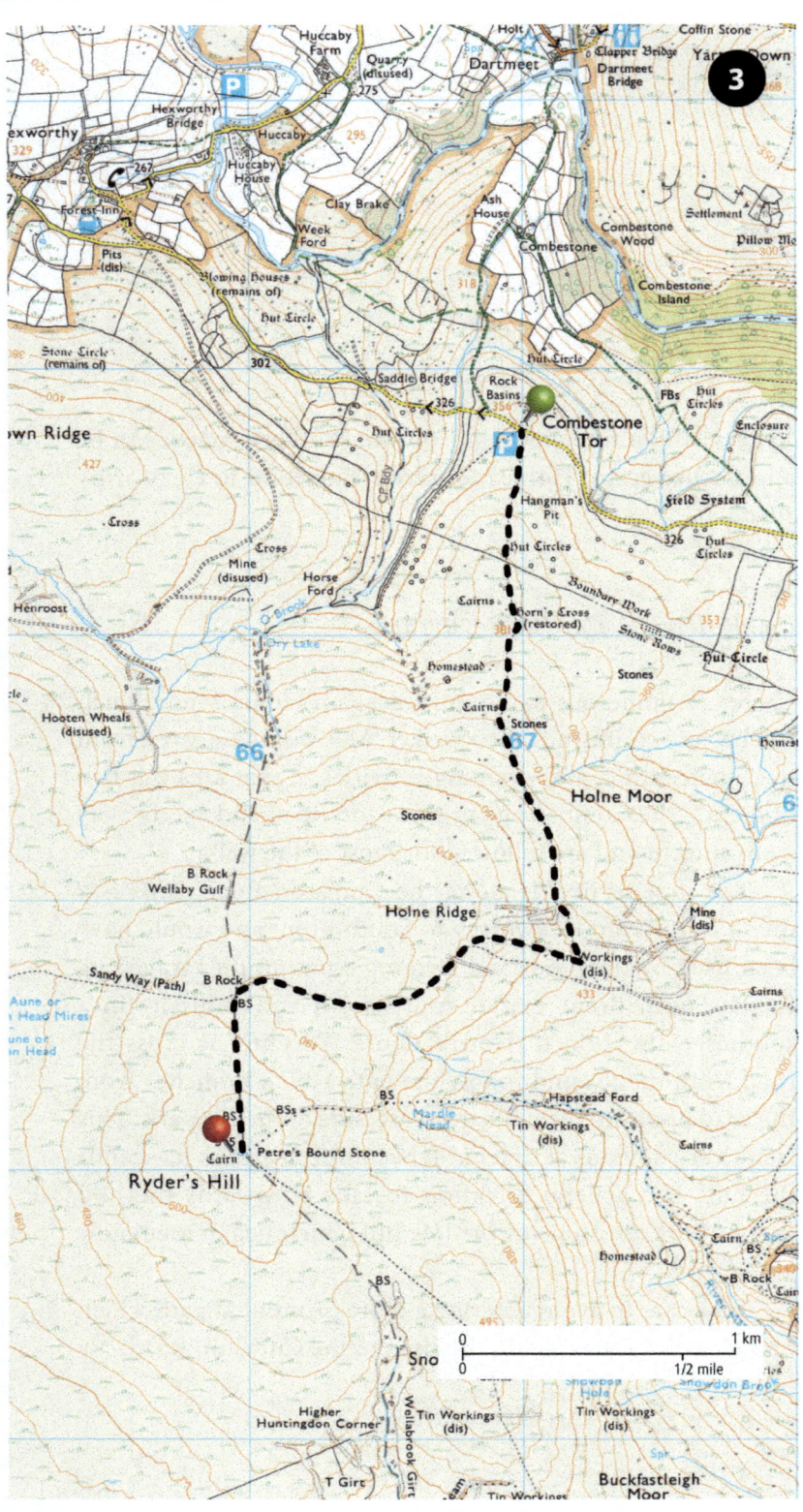

When the Cumston road forks after a short distance, take the left branch. This passes through an area of bracken and runs through a complex system of reaves, bending slightly to the left to avoid crossing one of these structures.

Soon Horn's Cross (670710) comes into view. This is one of the long line of crosses marking the Monk's Path or Maltern Way across the moor although this is not seen as a track here. The cross has an ancient head and was restored with a modern shaft. It is tall and seen easily from some distance around making it a most useful marker point for walkers.

Various paths converge here. The Cumston Road continues up the hill in a direct line with its approach to the cross. Immediately to the right of where it leaves the latter is a narrower path with a flat stone lying across it which may also be followed since it rejoins the Cumston Road further up the ridge.

As the Road ascends the ridge a stone marked PUDC, which is associated with the nearby Paignton reservoir, is seen about 50 yards to the right. The way bends to the left and passes above a deep valley, left, with views of the reservoir and the Dart Valley beyond. Soon the earthworks of the nineteenth century Ringleshutes tin mine are seen ahead and the way descends to a crossing of a mine gully (671700) and then ascends, past some mining earthworks, to two more PUDC stones which are about 40 yards apart. (The right stone is at 672698).

Leave the Cumston Road here and turn right to follow a green path which runs roughly parallel to a mine gully, right. Near the head of the gully (669699) where the track forks, take the left branch. A little further on the way meets another path (668699) which is entered, left. Some tinners' mounds are to be seen just beyond the intersection.

The route now joins that of the Sandy Way. This old path provided a route from Holne and Scoriton to the east end of Fox Tor Mire, south of Princetown. Three more gullies are crossed and beyond the third of these the path forks again (666696)where the right branch is taken. The head of the Mardle valley is on the left. Turn right and continue through what is now rather wild country. The way, often wet in places, runs alongside a large gully, right, and is followed to a point (65955 69657) where a path branches, left. There is a boundary stone here known as Fieldfare or Filfer Head, a short distance to the left, with an inscribed letter H. Look out for this carefully as it is quite small and leaning forward. This and other similar stones mark the boundary between the parish of Holne and the Dartmoor Forest.

Leave the Sandy Way here and take the path to the left which follows the parish boundary to the summit of Ryders Hill. As the top is approached, another boundary stone, known as Little Anthony is passed, right, which also has the letter H inscribed on one face.

Ryders Hill (660691) is a superb viewpoint with vistas in many directions of both the moor and the South Devon coastline with the Cornish coast to the west. Besides a trig point there are two stones on the summit. The taller of these, known as Petre's Boundstone, has the inscribed letter B and marks the point where Buckfastleigh and Holne parishes meet the Forest. The other stone is a modern replacement for a stone which disappeared known as Petre on the Mount inscribed with the letter H.

Return by the same route.

4

Huntingdon Warren and Broadafalls – 5½ miles

Walks 4 and 5 are over Buckfastleigh moor with some riverside sections through the upper Avon Valley. They form a pair of adjoining walks and if desired parts of them may be interchanged.

Walk 4 crosses the moor to the delightful cascade of Broadafalls (Broad Falls on OS map) on the Avon, returning along the river valley.

Start
Small roadside parking area (693672) a few hundred yards south of the lodge of Hayford Hall, on the Cross Furzes to Lud Gate road west of Buckfastleigh. This can be unsuitable for parking when the ground is wet when parking at Cross Furzes (700666) is advised (for details see walk 5).

The tarmac road terminates at the entrance to the Hayford Hall Lodge and continues to Lud Gate (684873) as a stony track. This runs between high banks and is an attractive approach to the moor, especially when the wild flowers are in bloom. Pass through the gate and continue on the track ahead, ignoring a bridle path, right, to Chalk Ford on the River Mardle. The track, which leads to Huntingdon Warren, is a little confusing for the first few hundred yards as it divides into two or three paths

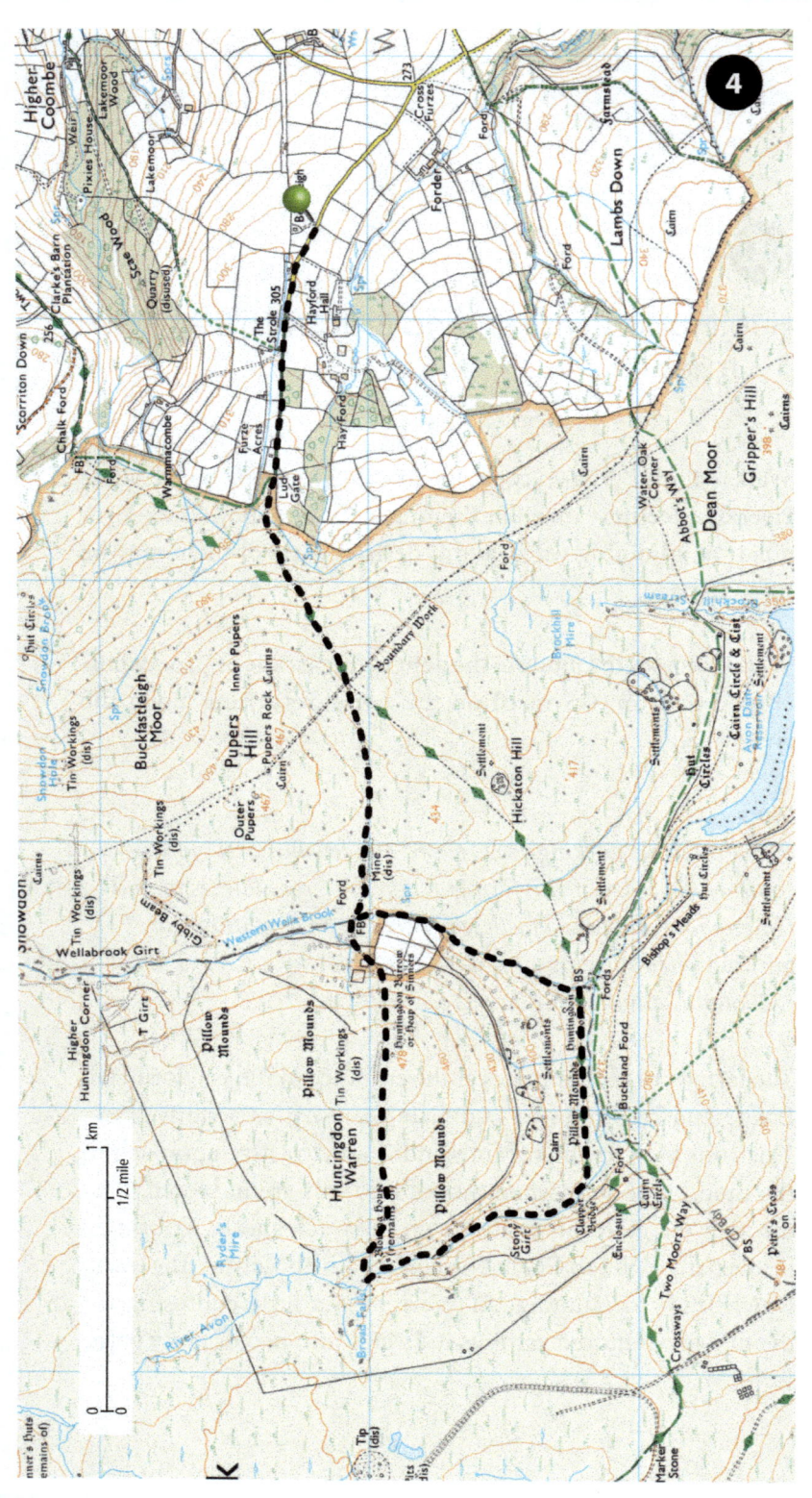

amongst gorse bushes, but the general direction is indicated by the stone wall which runs roughly parallel to the tracks a short distance away on the left.

The wall soon takes a right angle bend to the left. Here, between the track and the wall among some gorse bushes, is a holed stone. This is situated on the side of an old leat and was used to control the water flow when this was in use.

Ascend the track as it runs uphill, making for a point to the left of the hill summit. If any confusion arises as to which track to follow, the general direction can be checked by aligning the ascent with an imaginary projection of the wall from the gate. Take care not to enter a track which forks to the left about 100 yards above the wall right angle bend.

The track is followed to Huntingdon Warren. On the left, near the highest point of this section, is a small standing stone known as Little Man. About 200 paces further on another track, the Cumston Road (see walk 3) is crossed (676671). On the hill to the right are the Pupers Rocks.

On the hill to the left in the distance is a curiously shaped cairn, Eastern Whittabarrow, with a tower-like structure on top. It is said that the tower was built in the nineteenth century by a Paignton man so that he could see it from his house! Turn round and survey the fine view. Buckfast Abbey is seen in the valley way below and a wide area of South Devon is visible including, on a clear day, many miles of the coastline including the Teign Estuary and Torbay with Berry Head.

Continuing along the track the enclosures of the former settlement of Huntingdon Warren soon come into view, a large sycamore tree marking the spot where the warren house once stood. Gullys made by the tinners are to be seen on the hillside above the warren and further to the left on the same hill are warrener's buries. There are many of these on this hill which stand out very clearly when viewed from Google Earth. Descend the hill to a stream, the Wallabrook, a tributary of the Avon. On the descent to the left are some deep depressions which were air shafts of the nineteenth century Huntingdon Tin Mine of which extensive remains are passed on the approach to the stream.

The track crosses the Wallabrook by a small clapper bridge and then ascends obliquely to the left to reach the site of the Warren House (665669). This was sadly destroyed by fire in the 1960s. The last warrener and his wife, Mr and Mrs Waye, were there until the 1940s after which a hermit, Mr Symes, lived there until shortly before its destruction. I once met Mrs Waye and we had an interesting conversation about her life at this remote spot.

The walls of the field enclosures of the warren were in a semi-ruinous state for many years but were restored in the 1990s. I once spent a night here, the only time I have slept in the open on Dartmoor.

The next stage of the walk is up the hill immediately above the warren, making for a cairn on the summit known as Huntingdon Barrow or the Heap of Sinners (662669). There is a path over this section which is entered through a gate immediately to the right of the warren house remains. This runs to the right of a mound just above the warren and then to the left of a gully as it ascends the hill. At the top of the hill the path continues to the right of the cairn and left of some mounds. The view from here extends well into the southern Dartmoor wilderness area. Ahead and beyond the Avon Valley below is seen a large conical shaped mound. This is spoil from the former Redlake clay works which were abandoned in the early 1930s.

There is a path, which is now followed, from the cairn to the river above Broadafalls. This takes the walker through some rather rough ground; the general direction being towards the Redlake tip which is a useful point to steer by should the path be missed. On the right on the descent are some flat stones which provide a useful seat for those who wish to pause and survey the scene ahead. Some large rocks in the riverbed indicate the position of the falls (653670). The path disappears a short distance before reaching the river.

Broadafalls is one of those gems to be found high up on some of Dartmoor's rivers where the water takes a plunge over large boulders from the miry area of the high moor into the deep valleys. I like to stop here for a picnic and this is an ideal place to ponder and take in the wild beauty of the moor.

The return walk is along a path which runs along the left bank of the Avon to Huntingdon Cross. Just below the falls, a short distance from the left bank, is a tinners' blowing house. The valley below Broadafalls is very beautiful, especially when the heather is in full bloom. The path passes between two parallel stones, the sides of a warrener's vermin trap used to catch stoats and weasels which threatened to attack the rabbits. Upright slots on the inner sides of the stones accommodated shutters which were closed by a trip mechanism as the unfortunate animals passed through.

The vermin trap is by the only tree between Broadafalls and a two-span clapper bridge (657662) which crosses the river near where the latter changes course to adopt an easterly direction. The clapper was built by a warrener in the nineteenth century and is very useful to walkers – the Two Moors Way crosses here and I have incorporated it into walk 6.

Continue along the riverside path to Huntingdon Cross (664661). Along this section a pound, known as Biller's Pound, is seen on the hillside ahead. The cross lies beyond a stone wall which is crossed by a stile near the river. It is one of the four crosses erected at the time of the dissolution of the monasteries to mark the boundary of the Manor of Brent which came into the possession of Sir William Petre.

The Wallabrook, which was seen earlier at Huntingdon

Warren, joins the Avon here. Cross the brook which does not present any difficulty except in very wet weather when it may be necessary to seek a crossing place further up its valley. This is done conveniently opposite the mound and chapel described below.

Above the left bank of the Wallabrook, a few hundred yards upstream from the cross, is a ruined building which was the wheel pit of the Huntingdon Mine. Walk past the right side of this and make for a large raised area. In a dip in this is the Keble Martin Chapel (666666) which was built by some clergymen who used to meet here in the early years of the last century. Mrs Waye recalled these occasions when I met her and told me how they used to meet in June or July and put up camp. She said that she used to bake bread at the Warren House for them and take them milk. One of the clergymen was Rev Keble Martin who became famous late in life for his authorship of the *Concise British Flora*. The chapel consists of a small low-walled enclosure with stone seats at one end and an upright stone with an incised cross at the other. The roof is the sky!

From here take a route up the Wallabrook valley, where there are small paths, keeping about 100 yards above the stream and well above the rough ground of the mine workings, including a deep pit, to rejoin the Huntingdon Warren to Lud Gate track back to the start.

5

Abbot's Way to the Avon Valley – 5½ miles

This is another walk on Buckfastleigh Moor and the Avon Valley, taking in the eastern end of the Abbot's Way and a section of the Cumston Road.

Start

Cross Furzes west of Buckfastleigh where roads from Buckfast and Buckfastleigh meet at a T junction (700666). There is limited parking here at the side of the road from Buckfast. (Note: the name Cross Furzes is shown on the OS map beside a fork in the road (699668) a short distance to the north west of the T junction.)

Take the stony track which branches from the T junction opposite the Buckfast road and runs south west to the moor. This descends steeply into a wooded valley to cross a stream, the Dean Burn, by a two-span clapper bridge (698665). Dates are inscribed on each of the stone spans; 1705 on the first and 1872 on the other. However these have become partly obscured in recent years.

Cross the bridge just beyond which the track forks. Go straight ahead, through a gate beneath some large trees, and follow the path uphill across Lambs Down to the small conifer plantation of Water Oke Corner (686660). This section of the walk is a clearly defined path marked with guide posts. Signs

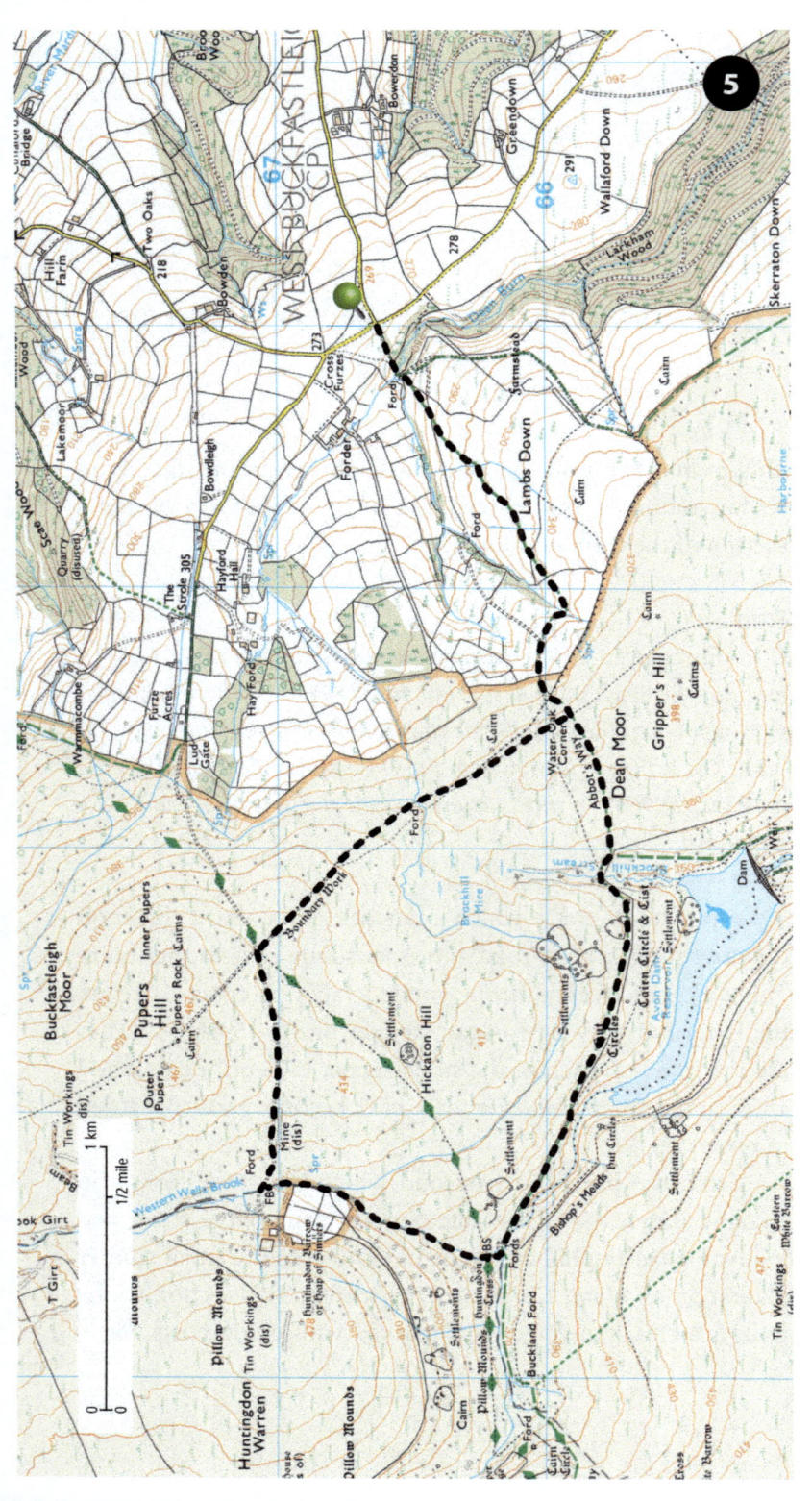

say keep to the path as this is private land. A few hundred yards before reaching the plantation the way bends to the right and descends to cross a stream, a tributary of the Dean Burn.

The path passes through a gate and enters the open moor, running initially parallel to the trees from which it is separated by a deep gully. It then continues straight ahead, after 150 paces crosses the Cumston Road, and ascends the ridge with the summit of Grippers Hill to the left.

On reaching the top of the ridge the Avon Valley comes into view with the reservoir and dam diagonally to the left. Straight ahead, on the hill beyond the valley, is the cairn of Eastern Whittabarrow (see walk 4).

The path then descends to Brockhill Ford where there is an easy crossing of this Avon tributary. From here the way is a substantial track, although rough in places, which runs upstream above the river to Huntingdon Cross. A short distance beyond the ford is a cist (678657) which is in a poor state of preservation: the two side stones have fallen inwards across the burial chamber. There are pounds and hut circles either side of the track, some of which were inundated when the reservoir was built. I visited this valley in the 1950s before the filling of the reservoir and took some photographs of the area about to be submerged including a fine tinners' blowing house with mould and mortar stones. These sometimes reappear in dry weather when the water level in the lake is very low. Also now under the water and occasionally visible is a monastic settlement which was probably the seasonal dwelling of the lay brothers from Buckfast Abbey. These sites were excavated by the archaeologist Lady Aileen Fox before the flooding took place.

Just before arriving at the cross the track passes Biller's Pound which is a short distance up Hickaton Hill, to the right. There are in fact two pounds here, Biller's being the largest with a very substantial surrounding bank. The other has only part of the pound wall remaining. There are several hut circles close together outside and to the west of Biller's Pound.

The Wallabrook flows into the Avon just before reaching Huntingdon Cross. The history of the cross is explained in the description of walk 4. The Abbot's Way, which crosses the Avon here, is now left behind and the walk continued by striking up the Wallabrook Valley to meet the Lud Gate to Huntingdon Warren track along the route, described for walk 4. Turn right into this track and follow it to where it crosses the Cumston Road (676671) (see walk 4). The Pupers Rocks are on the hill to the left.

Turn right into the Cumston Road which runs alongside a prehistoric reave. It descends to cross over the head of the Dean Burn and continues to join the outward route at the intersection with Abbots Way south west of Water Oke Corner.

Western Whittabarrow – 7½ miles

This walk follows the Zeal Tor Tramroad to Western Whittabarrow, returning along the Abbot's Way.

The tramroad was built in the mid-nineteenth century to carry peat from near Redlake in the upper Erme Valley to a treatment works near Shipley Bridge. This undertaking did not last long and the tramroad was later used for transport of men and materials in connection with a china clay undertaking at Petre's Pits, Bala Brook head.

Start
Shipley Bridge Car Park (681629) north west of South Brent. On the west side of the car park are the remains of the clay works including the settling tanks to which the clay suspended in water was brought down by a leat.

The easiest way to reach the tramway is to walk along the road which runs beside the river upstream to the Avon Dam. After ¼ mile a road to the Avon Water Treatment Works branches sharply to the left. Follow this which ascends steeply to the entry of the works enclosure (678630). The tramway is joined near here where it runs initially north west of west alongside a wall. However here it passes through an area of gorse bushes which can be difficult to negotiate. To avoid these enter the moor

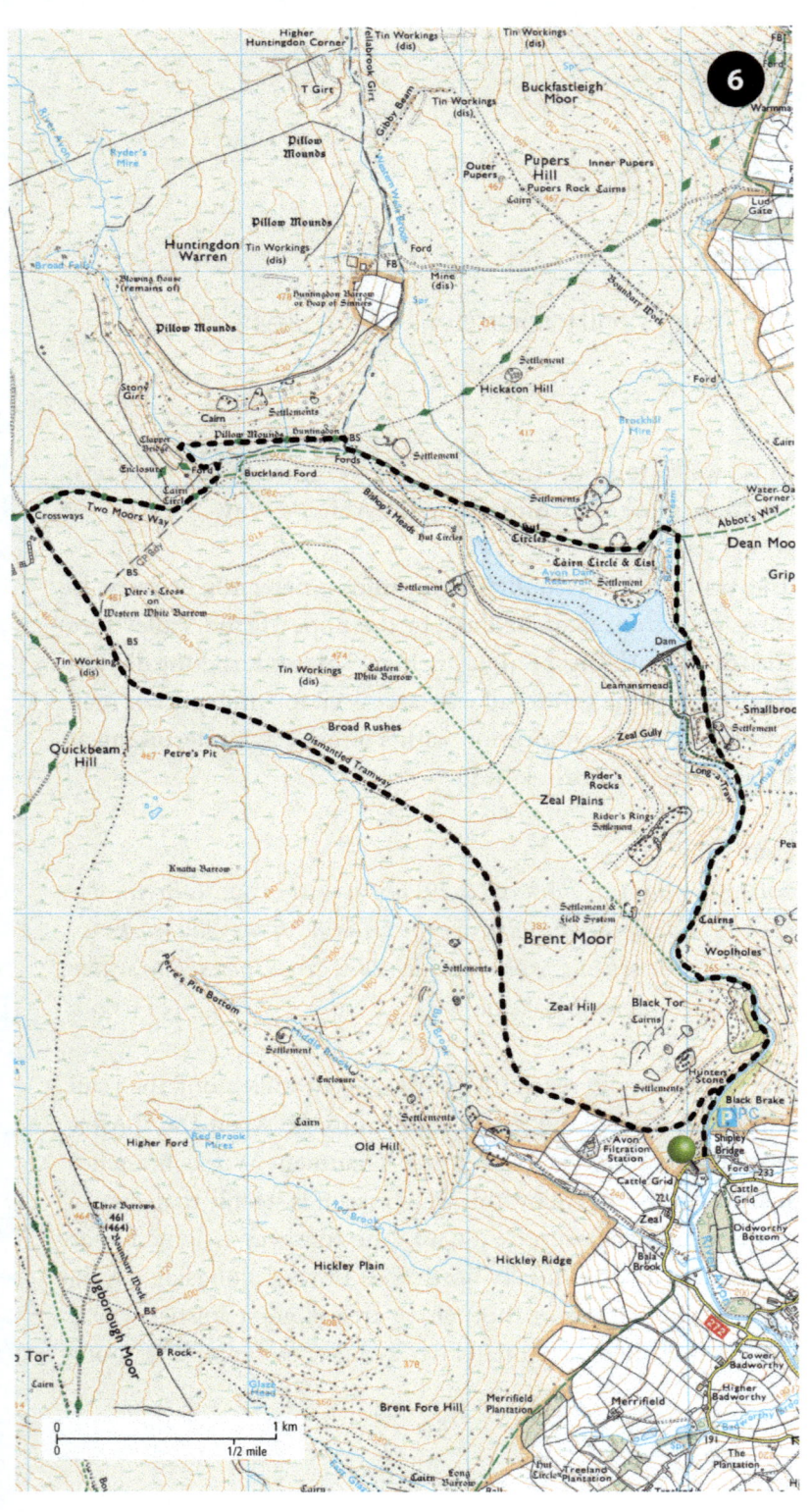

by turning right about 50 paces short of the works enclosure entrance and after a few yards turn left to take a course on the right of the tramway which is reasonably clear. When the end of the wall is reached turn left and walk for a few yards to meet the track of the tramway as it enters the open moor.

The tramway had wooden rails spiked to granite sets. These are long gone and the route is a clear track and an excellent route for walkers ascending to its terminus near Western Whittabarrow. There are fine views to the left over the Bala Brook Valley. At one point, near Bala Brook Head, where the stream passes through the former clay workings, the tramway has disintegrated to some extent, but a clear path remains which can be negotiated with care. Avoid taking a path which forks to the left into the valley near this point. Shortly beyond this the course of the tramway is made clear by the presence of a ¾ mile stone.

The tramway now passes through some wild country. The cairn of Western Whittabarrow (654655) comes into view on the right. On this are the remains of Petre's Cross, sadly denuded of its arms and planted upside down among the stones. This is one of the four crosses established by Sir William Petre (see Huntingdon Cross walk 4). The peat workers built a small house on the cairn of which the remains are still to be seen. They lived in this during the week, returning to their homes in the weekends. Crossing, in his *Guide to Dartmoor*, states that men who worked there had told him of the large number of rabbits they had seen prepared for dinner or supper. Huntingdon Warren provided a ready source of these. Continue along the tramway, passing, on the left, the remains of a small clay works building and china clay settling tanks associated with the clay workings at Redlake.

Some earth mounds, old clay workings, are now seen on the right and just beyond these the tramway crosses the Abbot's Way, which here is also the Two Moors Way, at a point known as Crossways (650659). Turn right to enter this which is now followed into the Avon Valley. A small clayworkers hut is seen on the right, and the way continues, passing to the left of a deep and massive tinners gert known as Pipers Beam.

On approaching the river at Buckland Ford the Abbot's Way followed the right bank downstream for a little under ½ mile to cross by a ford at Huntingdon Cross. However, although that ford may have been acceptable to wool jobbers or monks, it is too deep and dangerous for modern day walkers! Instead, on meeting the river, walk for a short distance upstream to cross by Huntingdon clapper and then walk downstream to the cross just beyond a boundary wall of the Huntingdon Warren enclosures which is crossed by a stile (this section is also part of walk 4).

Here the Wallabrook feeds into the Avon. This stream is usually easy to negotiate, but in case of difficulty walk up it to a higher point to find a more suitable crossing place. The Abbot's Way is rejoined and now follows the left side of the river. It is here a very substantial track, although rough in places. Pass through a valley known as Bishop's Meads to meet the Avon Reservoir. The track bends to the left to cross the Brockhill Stream, an Avon tributary, at Brockhill Ford. (The section between Huntingdon Cross and the ford is taken in the reverse direction in walk 5). After crossing the stream leave the Abbot's Way and follow a path which forks to the right. This runs above the Avon Dam to meet a tarmac road leading back to the start.

The route along the road is an attractive finish to the walk with fine river scenery. Black Tor is seen above the valley near which the road crosses the river and bends, with the river, to the left and then right. The ruins of Brent Moor House, a one time youth hostel, are seen on the right. Here the river runs over flat stones and especially when in spate, is a very impressive sight. There are also many rhododendron bushes which when in flower add to the beauty of this delightful spot.

7

Three Barrows – 5½ miles

This is a walk to the summit of Three Barrows, a fine viewpoint on southern Dartmoor, returning through the West Glaze Valley.

Start
Peak Moor Gate (677593) north of Wrangaton near South Brent where there is limited parking.

Enter the moor through the gate and follow the track which runs parallel to a stone wall, right. After about ½ mile at a point known as Owley Corner (670597), the wall bends sharply to the right and the path divides. Here there is a fine view of the wooded valley of the River Glaze. Continue ahead for a few yards to meet another track. This is the Plympton – Buckfast Monastic Way, linking Buckfast Abbey with the priory at Plympton. It is followed, left, up the ridge for about a mile with the Scad Brook valley, a tributary of the Glaze, on the right.

As the summit of the ridge is approached, a cross (659599) comes into view. This is Spurrell's Cross which marks the intersection of the monastic route and the Blackwood Path, an old peat cutter's track from Wrangaton to Erme Pound high up the Erme Valley. The romantic may imagine monks and peat cutters meeting here and passing the time of day, but

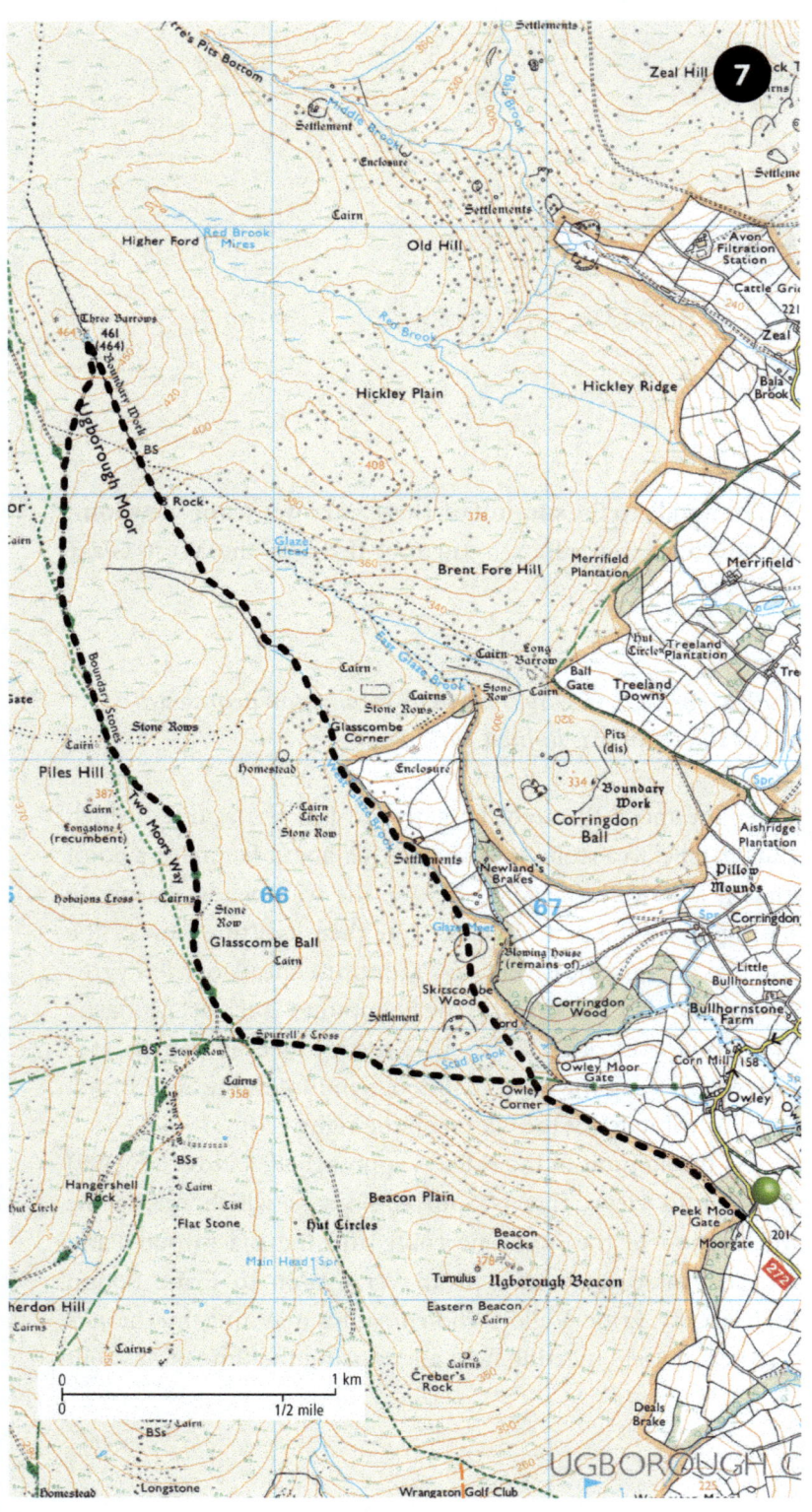

somehow I think this is in the realms of fantasy! Both tracks, which intersect a few yards beyond the cross, are very clear here and this is an impressive example of an ancient cross forming a marker for the moorland traveller. The head of the cross lay flat on the moor for many years and was re-erected on a modern shaft by the Dartmoor Preservation Association. One arm is missing but an interesting feature is the projecting spurs that project from the top and remaining arm. There is a short stone row a short distance to the south west of the cross.

Turn right into the Blackwood Path, which here is sunken, for a short distance to reach the track of the former Redlake Railway. This was opened in 1911 to connect the Redlake china clay works in the upper Erme Valley with the Great Western main line at Bittaford. It carried general freight for the works as well as the workmen but the clay itself was conveyed by pipeline in an aqueous suspension. By 1932 the best clay had been exhausted and the works and railway closed. Turn right to join this which is followed to where the short path to the summit of Three Barrows forks to the right (652621).

There are several interesting prehistoric remains in this area including the Butterdon Hill stone row which lies a short distance to the left (west) of the railway. Beyond the northern end of this is a stone (655605) which has an incised cross, known as Hobajon's Cross. North of this are two standing stones (654607), the smaller of which is a modern boundary marker and the larger a menhir.

Another stone row, of which most of the stones are fallen no attempt having been made to re-erect them, crosses the tramway at (654611). This is unusual in that it runs across the ridge from east to west, rather than north–south like the other major rows in this area.

Follow the path to Three Barrows (653627), which, as its name implies, is a group of three cairns or barrows which crown the hill summit. On a clear day the views from here extend southwards to much of the South Devon coast and into Cornwall. In the opposite direction the wild character of the southern Dartmoor Wilderness is very apparent and there are fine views westwards into the Erme Valley and beyond and to the east the valley of the Avon and its tributaries.

The return route follows a prehistoric reave, marked on the OS map as boundary work, into the valley of the West Glaze. This is joined on the south west side of Three Barrows, a few yards to the west of the southernmost cairn and terminates near the stream at 657617. Then walk downstream along the left bank to a spot known as Glasscombe Corner (663610). There is a ford here and a small group of trees. This is the upper limit of enclosures on the left side of the river, whereas the land on the right side continues as open moorland.

Cross the stream and continue down the valley above the right bank where there is much evidence of tinners' activities. The path divides from where the corner of the wall at Owley Corner can be seen. Take the lower path which passes through a prehistoric pound. The near, northern embankment of the settlement is clear, with bracken and a few trees along its length. The path enters the enclosure around ten yards from the western edge, marked by the most westerly tree of those on the embankment. It then crosses the pound and descends to cross the Scad Brook which is easily negotiated except after heavy rain and continues to meet the outward route.

An alternative route from Glasscombe Corner is to walk beside the river by descending into the wooded gorge through which it flows. This leads to Glazemeet, a beautiful spot where the East and West Glaze unite. A short distance below this point, beside the river, is a tinners' blowing house among the ruins of which is a quadruple mortar stone.

Near here the river passes over a waterfall and through a deep pool. This was named the Wishing Pool since it was alleged that a wish made whilst leaping across it would be granted. However one glance at the pool reveals that this would be no mean feat even to an olympic athlete and it is not recommended! It should be said, however, that this romantic name is more likely to have been derived from the word 'watering'.

The route below this point runs over some wet ground which needs careful negotiation, crossing the Scad where it flows into the Glaze and then proceeding along a path diagonally to the right to reach Owley Corner. The route of outward walk is then taken to the start.

8

Piles Copse – 3½ miles

Piles Copse beside the river Erme, one of Dartmoor's three ancient oak woods, is a delightful and tranquil place to visit and an ideal destination for those seeking a short walk among fine moorland, woodland and river scenery.

Start
Harford Moor Gate (644595) north of Ivybridge, where there is car parking space in and around a small disused gravel pit.

From the car park turn left and enter a track which runs near a wall from which it gradually diverges to run about twenty paces from it. Ignore a path which branches off to the right to ascend the ridge and another running beside the wall. Beyond where the wall bends to the left the path runs uphill across the open moor before descending to enter a gate into a large enclosure known as Lower Piles. The fine scenery of the middle Erme Valley comes into view and Piles Copse is now visible. On the far side of the valley is the lofty ridge of Stalldon beyond which is Penn Beacon. Nearer the river, also on the far side, is a small tor known as Tristis Rock.

On the descent to the gate, on the right, is a fine cist (645603). I was once told of a lady who, standing by it, said how she would like to be buried there on which she fell in!

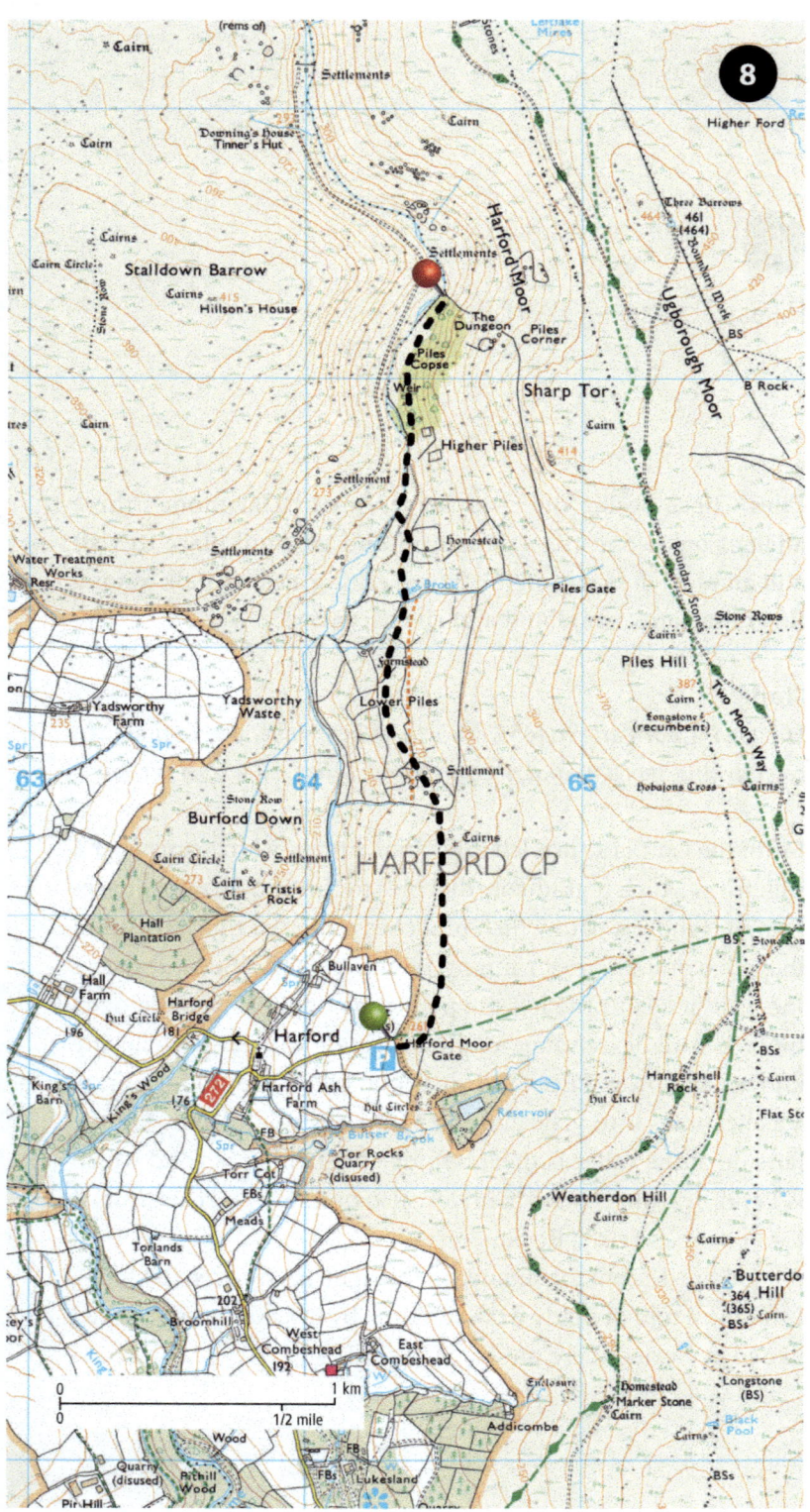

Pass through the gate (645604) and follow the track which bends initially to the left. Bluebells flower here in the late spring, a beautiful sight. There is an interesting complex of hut circles here with a network of interconnecting walls which it has been suggested formed small paddocks. The track leads on to near to another wall, left (ignore a branch which leads right up to the wall) and runs on to meet a gully through which runs the Piles Brook, a small tributary of the Erme. It then bends to the right, past a small corrugated iron building, right, to a gate (644612) through the northern wall of Lower Piles. It is necessary to cross the Piles Brook here which flows alongside the wall in front of the gate; this does not usually present any difficulty if normal care is taken.

Pass through the gate to enter the area known as Higher Piles which incorporates the wood. The track runs straight on and passes near a large square enclosure much overgrown with bracken, right, which has an exceptionally well preserved boundary wall, possibly because the original prehistoric structure was re-used in medieval times. The track then bends to the left, descends to the river and enters the wood. The latter starts at about grid reference 646614, rather further south than shown on the OS map.

There is no obvious path through the wood but a suitable way is easily found.

Return by the same route.

9

Trowlesworthy Bronze Age remains – *3 miles*

This is a short walk along a leat to view the Trowleswothy stone rows.

Start
Take the Trowlesworthy Warren Track which branches left off the road running south east and about ½ mile from Cadover Bridge, near Meavy. There is a parking area (563644) to the left of this track, just before it crosses the Blackabrook.

Follow the track east, crossing the Blackabrook bridge, which is just above the confluence of this stream with the Plym, and proceed to a point just short of the Trowlesworthy Warren House enclosures (566647). The ridge ahead is crowned by the Trowlesworthy Tors. Then turn left along a track which runs above the warren enclosures, parallel to the boundary wall. This can be muddy in wet weather!

    Continue to a fork near the far end of the enclosures and take the left branch which runs uphill to a bridge over a leat (572647). This is the Lee Moor Leat which picks up water from the River Plym below Ditsworthy Warren (walk 10). Cross the bridge and turn right to follow the path for ½ mile along the leat's left, north west side. This is a pleasant walk, the leat flowing gently around the hillside. It is crossed at frequent intervals by little one span stone bridges which were placed there to aid

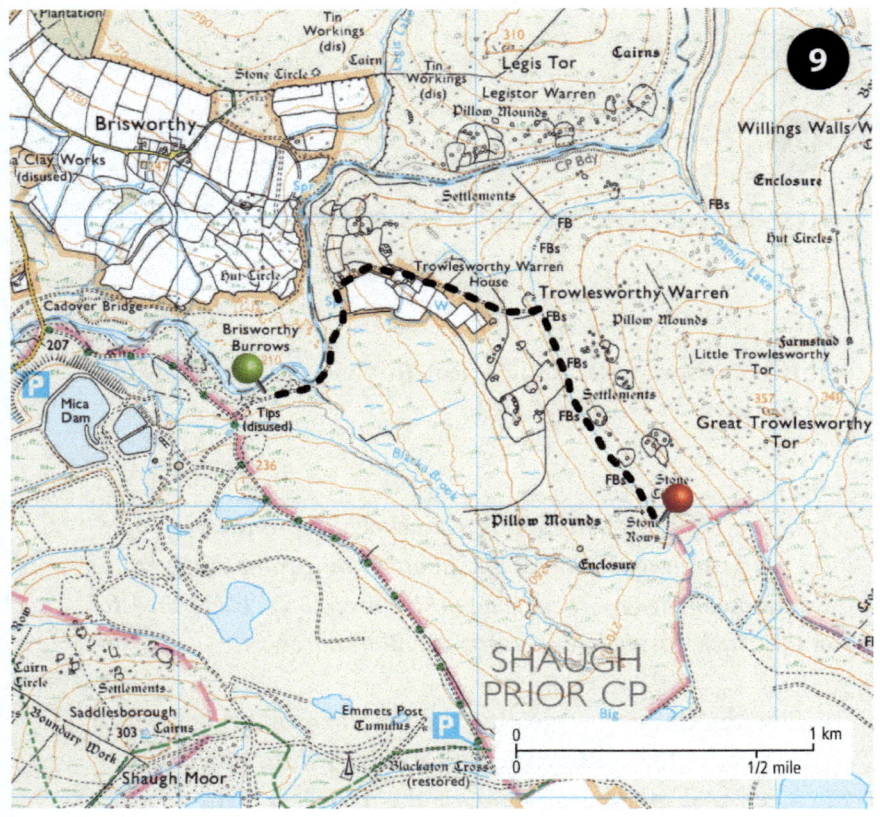

the warrening activities. There are a number of enclosures and hut circles on the moor to the left of the leat including a triple enclosure. To the right are the waste tips of the china clay works; these ugly intrusions on the Dartmoor scene have been softened to some extent by grassing them over.

On approaching the stone rows the ground is very marshy. To avoid this cross over a stone bridge and continue along the right bank of the leat for a short distance.

The rows are to be found here either side of the leat. To the right, west of the leat is a single row with a small menhir at the west end and the east end ending in a cairn. This row is oriented in an east west axis.

The other row, which lies in a south south west orientation, runs across the leat. This is a double row which terminates at its upper end in a fine stone circle of eight stones, known as the pulpit.

Return by the same route.

10

Ditsworthy Warren and Drizzlecombe – 3½ miles

This is a short walk to the Drizzlecombe Bronze Age complex, outward via Edward's Path, returning by the Ditsworthy Warren track.

Start
Below Gutter Tor (577673), east of Sheepstor. There is parking space for several cars on the right of the road near where the tarmac road terminates.

The first objective is Ditsworthy Warren House. This may be reached in one of two ways, either by following the stony warren track which is entered by walking back along the road for a few yards and then turning left, or across the moor via Edward's Path. I personally prefer the latter which is kinder to the feet and am suggesting this is followed for the outward walk.

For Edward's Path walk on from the tarmac road and continue ahead for a short distance on the stony track which leads to the former Eylesbarrow Mine. This crosses a stream, the Sheepstor Brook, a short distance beyond which is a small plantation on the right. Enter the gate (581674) into this and proceed through the trees past a building on the left known as Scout Hut. Pass through the gate on to the open moor and follow the path ahead.

For much of its length Edward's Path runs to the left of

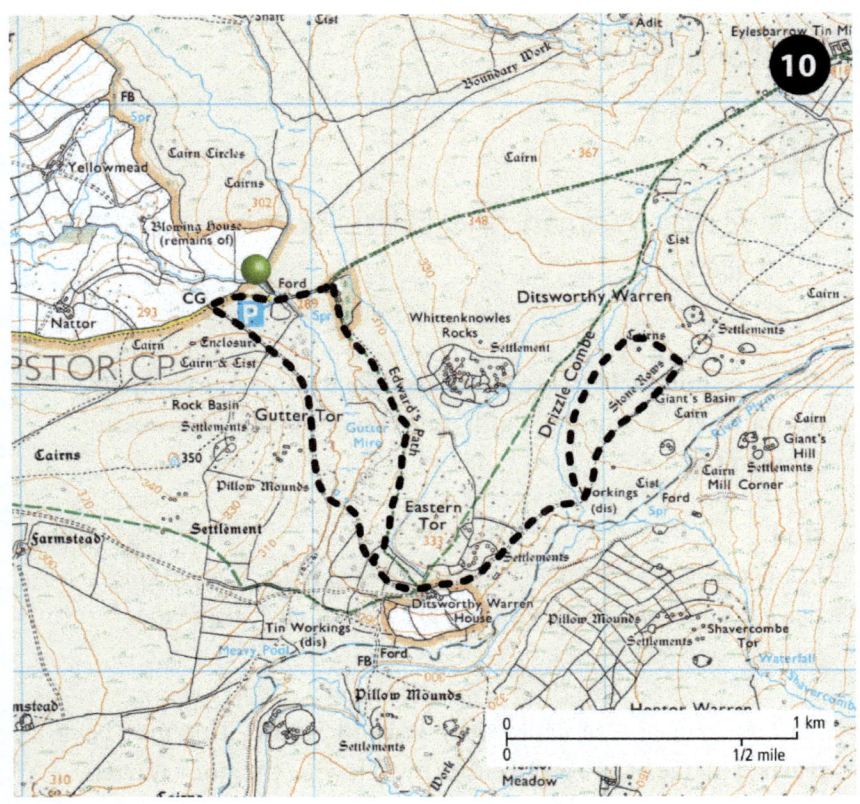

a boggy area, known as Gutter Mire. After a few hundred yards the path crosses a tinners' gully beyond which, rather than continuing along the route to the left, as shown on the OS map, turn right to meet the warren track. This is then entered and followed, left, to the Warren House (584667). Just before reaching the warren track is a long mound, one of many buries or pillow mounds built by the warreners for the rabbits to burrow in. Others are seen on the left as the warren is approached.

Ditsworthy, the largest of the Dartmoor warrens, was run

for many years by the Ware family, the last member of which, Mrs Nicholas Ware, continued there until her death in 1945. The house was used as the setting for the recent film War Horse.

In the walls of the enclosure at the back of the house are what appear to be three small caves. These were dog kennels, the enclosure being known as Kennel Court. The dogs were kept to round up the rabbits.

Continue along the track past the house which continues up the Plym valley, with the river below on the right. Cross a stream, the Thrushelcombe, a tributary of the Plym, at a ford (589666). There are fine views across the river, right, to the area around Hen Tor. This tor is unusually situated, being a rock outcrop on the side of the hill rather than on the summit. There is a complex field system between the tor and the river.

Ahead are seen three large upright stones, the menhirs of the Drizzlecombe Bronze Age monuments, a complex of burial and ceremonial structures of outstanding interest. The menhirs each terminate a stone row. There are a number of cairns, including a large one known as Giant's Basin.

To view the complex the following route is suggested. First note a cist a short distance ahead at 592676. Then walk diagonally to the left to the nearest menhir.

From here follow the stone row to the far end and view the other menhirs and rows. Giant's Basin lies to the left, north west of the rows. There is a structure, the probable remains of a small cist, on the south west of this cairn. A very impressive cist, marked cairns on the OS map, at (591671) lies north west of the complex and is easily spotted by its capstone which has been placed upright at the side of the burial chamber. To the north west of this is a rather unusual cairn which Hansford Worth (*Worth's Dartmoor*) describes as a kerb circle. It consists of adjoining stones around less than half the circumference.

For the return route return to the crossing of the Thrushelcombe stream and retrace the outward route to Ditsworthy Warren. Then either take Edward's Path or the Warren Track back to the start.

The Langcombe Valley and Grim's Grave – 5 miles

The Langcombe stream is a remote tributary of the River Plym and is noteworthy for the number of cists to be found there especially the large and impressive Grim's Grave. This walk follows a direct route to that area across the open moor returning via the Plym Valley. The route adjoins that of walk 10 and sections may thus be interchanged.

Start
Gutter Tor (577673), east of Sheepstor where there is a parking area for several cars adjacent to the right side of the road.

The car park is at the end of a tarmac road which continues as a track to the former Eylesbarrow tin mine. Follow this for ⅔ mile to where a path branches off to the right. This leads south east direct to Plym Steps just upstream from where the Langcombe joins the Plym. A stone marked PC WW 1917 seen on the left side of the Eylesbarrow track (590677) just before the path diverges is a useful indicator that the latter is approached.

    A glance at the OS map shows that the path soon crosses a track to Ditsworthy Warren which itself branches from the Eylesbarrow track. In the angle between the path and the Ditsworthy track is a rectangular enclosure.

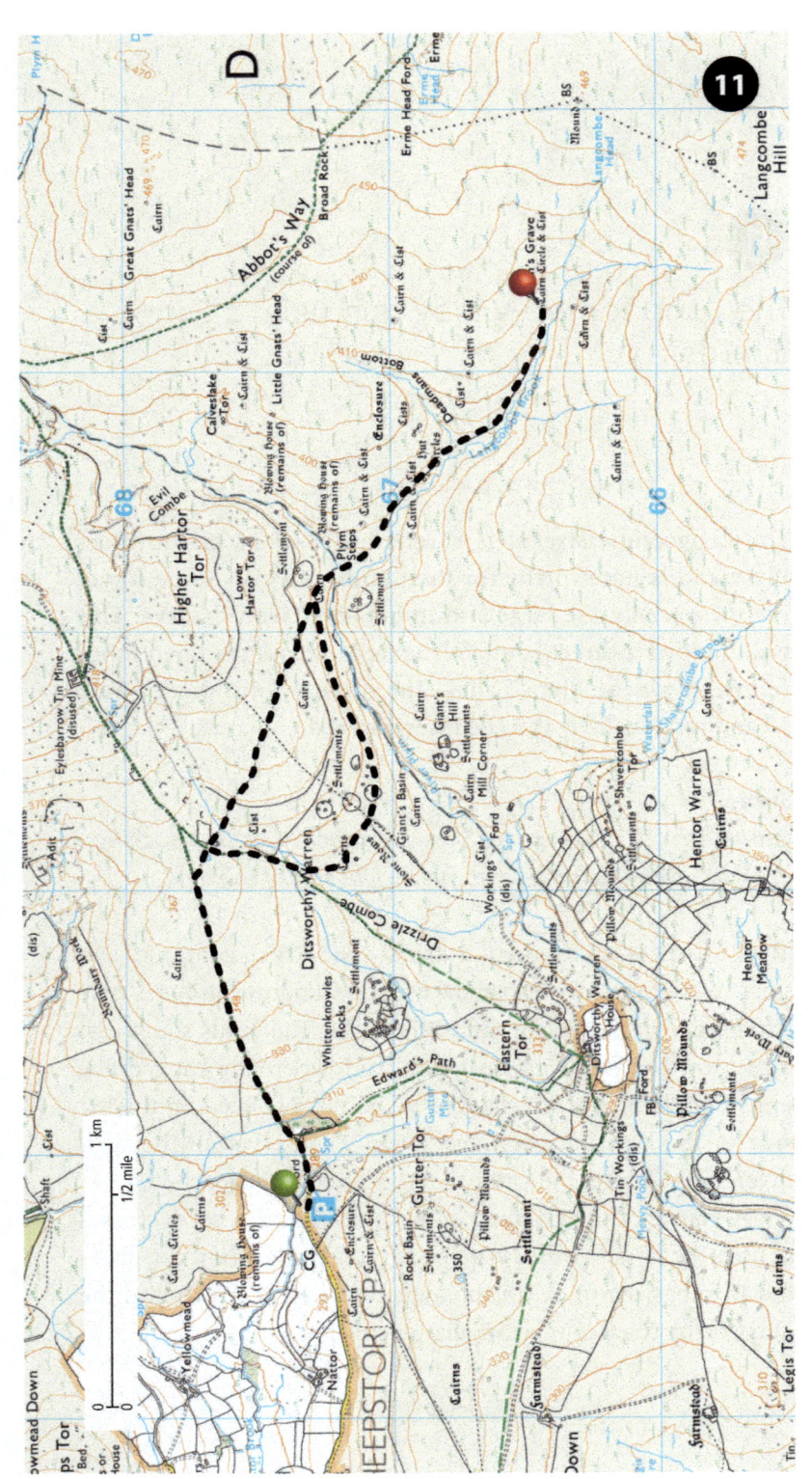

The path to Plym Steps is marked as a thin dotted line on the OS map and is visible on Google Earth. The course of it is not always clear and if it is missed at any point continue in a south east direction. The bank of a dry leat is soon crossed; this was the former Stamping Mill Leat which provided a source of power to the mills at Eylesbarrow Mine. The path then crosses another path (596675) running south west from below Higher Hartor Tor. Both Lower and Higher Hartor Tors are seen diagonally to the left and the Plym and Langcombe valleys come into view ahead.

The disused Stamping Mill Leat, which follows a route round the contours to the right, is now met again. The way bends to the left and then right to cross the leat. Then follow a course to join a track which descends to Plym Steps where there is a ford (603672). To reach the Langcombe valley cross the Plym here; there is a suitable crossing place a short distance downstream from the ford. The crossing is normally not difficult but requires care. There is a tinners' blowing house near the river a short distance upstream on the left bank.

From the ford the Langcombe is now on the right. Follow a path up the valley which runs quite close to this stream just above extensive tinners' workings. After ½ mile the path crosses a tributary, the Deadman's Bottom Stream, and continues to Grim's Grave which is another ½ mile up the valley and is seen a short distance across a green area to the left of the path at 612664.

Grim's Grave is a very impressive monument. The large cist has all four sides in place and a retaining circle of nine large stones. There are altogether eleven cists in the Langcombe valley and an interesting time can be had locating them with the aid of the OS map.

For the return walk return to Plym Steps and recross the river. To continue walk back along the outward track for about

85 paces to locate at 60226723 a path which branches to the left. This leads down the valley to the Drizzlecombe Bronze Age complex (walk 10). Where the path divides take the right branch to continue the path which runs alongside the right bank of the disused Longstone leat. This very long leat, which took its water supply from the Plym below Plym Steps, provided a water supply to Longstone Manor at Sheepstor.

Details of the Drizzlecombe complex are given in walk 10. To continue the present walk proceed to the tallest menhir and then in a north west direction to the large cist (591671), easily spotted by the capstone which has been displaced and left in a tilted position. Then join a path just beyond here which leads in a northerly direction to Jobber's Ford across the Thrushelcombe stream. There is another cist (592679) a short distance above the left bank of the stream.

The route from the Deadman's Bottom stream to Jobber's Ford follows the approximate course of the Buckland branch of the Abbot's Way / Jobber's Path.

Cross the stream at Jobber's Ford – this is easily done just upstream – and continue up the far bank to meet the Eylesbarrow to Ditsworthy track. Turn right and follow this to where it meets the outward route.

12
Nun's Cross from Burrator Lake – *5½ miles*

Nun's Cross, the oldest, tallest and probably the best known of these noble monuments on Dartmoor, stands at the intersection of two ancient tracks on the moor south of Princetown. In the present walk it is approached from Burrator Lake by walking over the slopes of Down Tor and along the ridge between the valleys of the Newleycombe and Narrator.

Start
Car park at Norsworthy Bridge (569693) above the north western end of Burrator Lake. There is a parking area among the trees on the east side of the road at this popular spot where the Newleycombe Lake joins the River Meavy.

The walk starts at a track running between moss covered walls which branches from the road at the southernmost point of the parking area. Enter this and then take a path which branches immediately to the left. Use of this by vehicles has been blocked by a line of rocks. It rises steadily through the trees to Down Tor (579694). In places it is a green way and it passes through field enclosures. There are fine views to the left across the wooded Newleycombe valley and beyond to Leather Tor.

After about ½ mile a large rock is seen ahead. Just before reaching this the path crosses a large gully (572693) and another

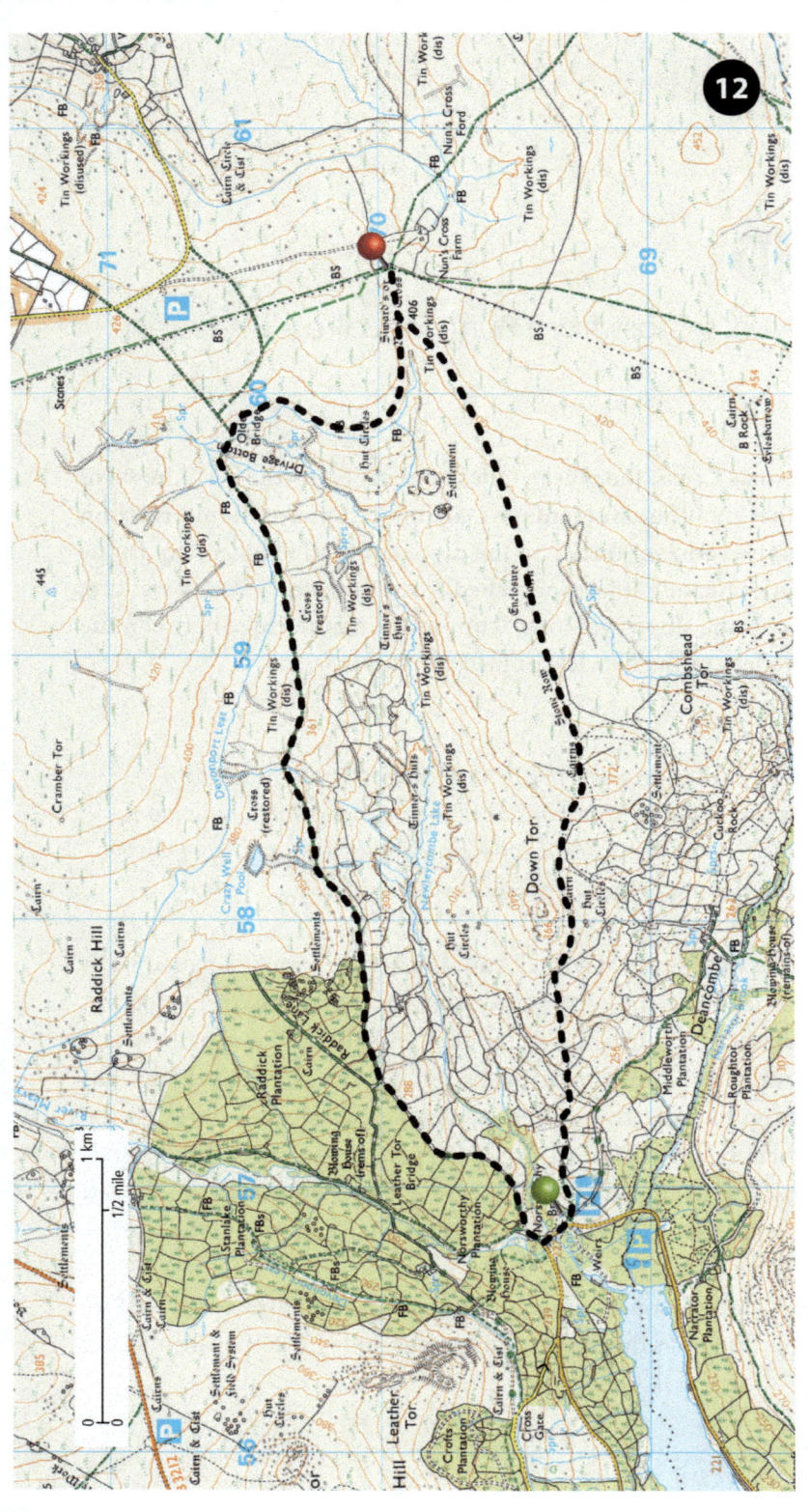

path branches to the left. Ignore the latter and carry on directly ahead, passing to the left of the rock, continuing to the base of the tor. The route continues round the right side of the tor. There is no obvious path here so take any suitable course, carefully negotiating the rocks.

Beyond the tor continue in an approximately south of east direction, passing to the left of a stone wall and then ascend Hingston Hill. A fine stone circle (587693) and row come into view. The circle, a large one, is at the near, west end of the row. The stones of the latter near the join with the circle are exceptionally large. Walk along the row to the east end; a path runs parallel with it on the left side. There is a blocking stone at the far end. Combestone Tor is seen to the south, right.

The next objective is Nun's Cross (605699) which is reached by walking along a path in a north east direction. A cairn and a pound are seen a short distance beyond the end of the row. The path runs to the right of the cairn and the way then ascends steadily to near the head of a branch of the Newleycombe Lake. Two trees close together and the ruins of a small building come into view, left.

The way bends to the left on approaching some mounds associated with the former Nun's Cross Tin Mine and the path taken for the return route is met (603699). To visit Nun's Cross turn right into the latter which passes through some more tinners' workings beyond which the cross comes into view. I once brought a walking group along here in the mist and the grey outline of the cross emerging was an evocative sight.

Nun's Cross lies at the crossing of the Tavistock branch of the Abbot's Way (Jobber's Path) and the Monk's Path which provides an alternative route for the east-west crossing of the moor. Nun's is one of the many crosses marking this route, the most easterly of which, Horn's Cross, is seen on walk 3. Its existence was recorded in 1240 to mark the bounds of the Dartmoor Forest (the sovereign's hunting preserve). There are incriptions on the cross – on the eastern face is the word SIWARD which may refer to Siward, Earl of Northumberland who owned extensive land in the Tavistock area in the reign of Edward the Confessor and on the west side of the shaft is inscribed 'BOC LAND' which may relate to the land west of the cross held by monks of Buckland Abbey. The shaft of the cross was broken in 1846 and was restored by securing with an iron clamp. The lonely Nun's Cross Farm house, now used as an adventure centre, is seen to the south east of the cross.

The return route follows more crosses which mark the route of the Monk's Path as it leads to the western border of the moor. To join this return to the junction of the two paths and follow the right fork which descends through further mounds. The trees noted from the outward path are seen, right and the Devonport Leat emerges on the left, in a deep gully, from the leat tunnel which runs under Nun's Cross Farm. Continue by taking the path along the right bank of the leat. A cross is passed near a leat maintenance hut. This is known as Hutchinson's Cross and is a modern one in an old socket hole. It was set up in 1968 by Lt Commander B. Hutchinson R.N. as a memorial to his mother Mrs S. L. Hutchinson and is inscribed with her initials 'S. L. H. 1887–1966'. Beyond the cross the leat runs over a waterfall.

The leat path continues to join the old stony track, Uncle's Road at Older Bridge (598706). Turn left into this and descend into the Meavy Valley. This section in the reverse direction is followed in walk 13. Newleycombe Cross (592703) which has a restored lower portion of the shaft lies on the left and Crazy Well Cross (not visible from the track) of which only the head and arms are original (583704), right. Crazy Well Pool can be visited by making a short deviation to the right of the track (see walk 13).

The track meets the extensive conifer plantations above Burrator Lake and runs downhill with the trees on the right. The track branches at 574700 with the right fork running into the plantation. Take the left branch which continues along the edge of the plantation back to the start.

13

Black Tor Falls and Crazy Well Pool – 6 *miles*

Princetown is the starting point for this walk which passes through part of the upper Meavy Valley, continuing along the Devonport Leat to Crazy Well Pool.

Start
Princetown; small car park (587733) on the left a short distance along the Yelverton Road, just beyond the last house. Alternatively park in the main car park in the village.

The first objective is Hart Tor, 1 mile away to the south west, reached by following a path which starts a short distance south west of the small car park. It runs downhill initially; there is a green area where it is indistinct for a short distance, after which it becomes clear again and runs uphill to the left, south east, side of the Tor. There are views ahead of Sheepstor, left and Sharpitor, right.

Walk left round the Tor to the south west side, descend in a south west direction into the River Meavy Valley to meet the upper end of a double stone row (577717) to which there is a path starting a short distance below the tor. Don't take a path on the left from the tor which descends to the Hart Tor Brook.

This is one of two stone rows, the other, a few yards to the south, being a single alignment. They both start in cairns with

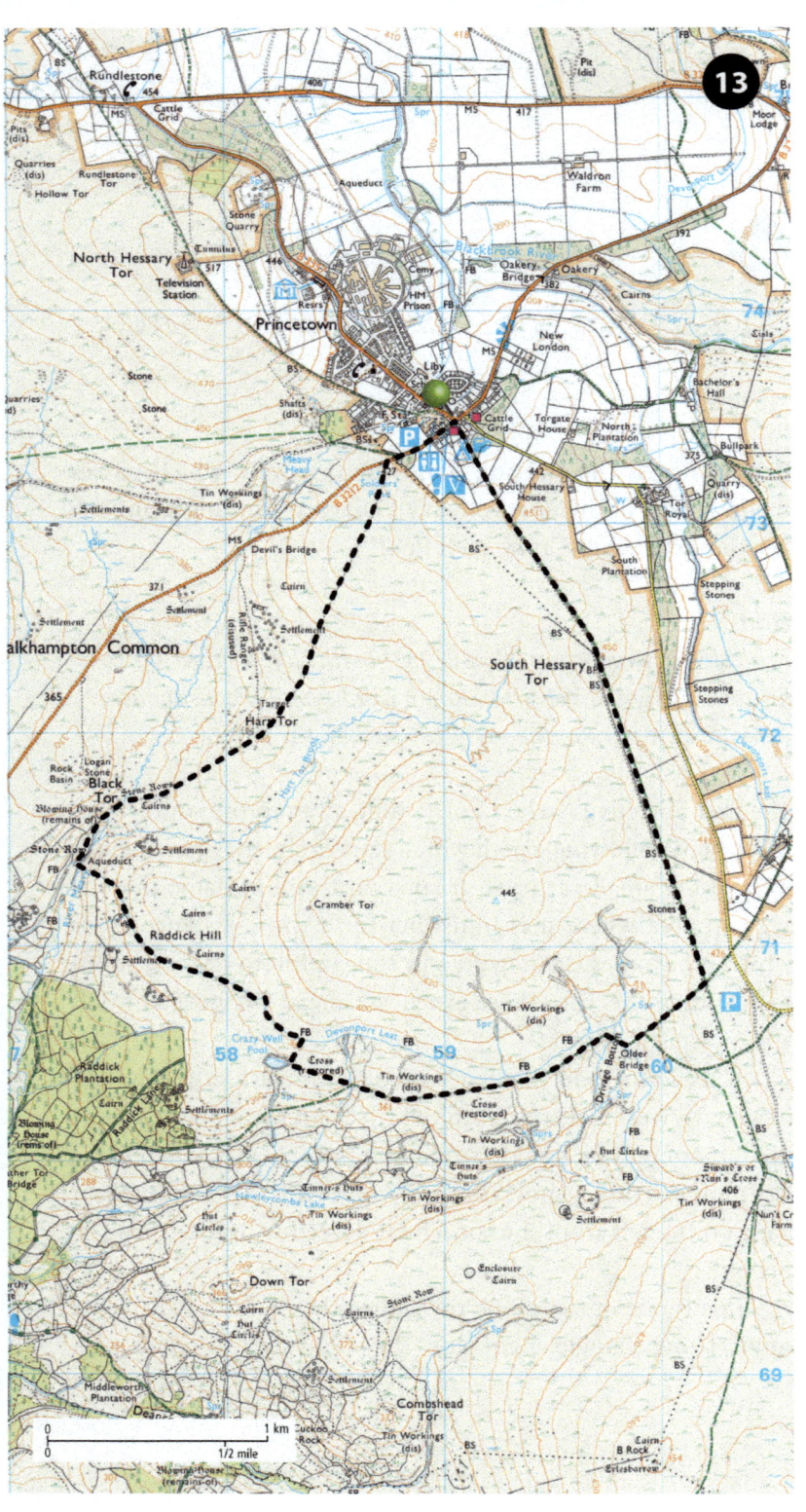

retaining circles and run down to near the river. The rows run alongside each other but are not quite parallel, diverging as they descend.

Walk down to the river bank to where the double row terminates near a ford (575717) and then for a short distance downstream to where the Meavy cascades over the imposing Black Tor Falls. There is some rough ground here due to tinners' workings and some wet areas which are easily negotiated with care. An interesting blowing house is to be seen beside the river below the falls (575716). This is relatively well preserved with a door lintel still in place. It bears the inscription XIII which Hansford Worth suggests may have some connection with the registration of the blowing houses. There are two mortar stones. I visited this spot for the first time in the summer of 1955, having travelled from Princetown on the train to Ingra Tor Halt and then walking across the moor in the mist.

To continue the walk it is necessary to cross the river to the right bank. It is normally relatively easy to step across a short distance below the falls and at the time of writing, there is a metal 'plank' (575716) which affords a reasonable bridge although this cannot be regarded as a permanent feature. There is another blowing house here above the right bank.

The route then runs downstream either by following a path near the river or climbing the bank to follow another path at a higher level, the latter being the easier route. An aqueduct carries the Devonport Leat which flows down the east side of the valley in an impressive cascade known as the Leat Falls. Cross the aqueduct and walk uphill on the path alongside the left of the falls. Continue along the leat, as it runs around the side of Raddick Hill, to where it makes a detour around a gully (582787). The forestry plantations above Burrator are passed, right. Just beyond the gully is a sluice gate and a short distance further on is a stone bridge (584706) where an ancient cart track crosses the leat. Cross here and walk for a short distance to Crazy Well Pool.

This famous pool, said to be bottomless, is an old mine working. It has been said that the level of the water in the pool rises and falls with the tide at Plymouth! It is in fact an attractive feature and a good spot for a refreshment break.

A short distance south east of the Pool is Crazy Well Cross (583704), one of the long line of these noble monuments marking the Monk's Path. From the cross walk on for a short distance downhill to meet the track known as Uncles' Road which is joined, turning left and followed to Older Bridge (598706). This section forms part of the return of walk 12. The valley of the Newleycombe Lake lies below to the right. Newleycombe cross is a short distance away on the right (592703).

The track crosses the Newleycombe stream at Older Bridge (598706) and, a few yards further on, the Devonport Leat. The route now ascends to meet the Tavistock branch of Jobber's Path (602708) which is taken, left, for a direct route, passing South Hessary Tor (597724), to the centre of Princetown.

Upper Plym Valley and Erme Head – 6½ miles

The high ground between the Plym and Erme Valleys, is a fine view point at the centre of the southern moor. This walk follows tracks which provide a continuous link to this remote spot from the Whiteworks road south of Princetown.

Start
Small car park (604708) on the Whiteworks road. There are two car parks here on the right side of the road quite close together; park in the second one which is just before the road bends to the left.

Take the track which leaves the road on the right immediately beyond the car park and runs south east of south to Nun's Cross Farm. There are extensive views from the track to the left across Fox Tor Mire and beyond.

Nun's Cross farmhouse, which like Huntingdon and Ditsworthy Warrens, was one of the really remote dwellings on Dartmoor. It was built in 1901 to supersede a more primitive building erected 30 years earlier when the surrounding land was enclosed. The house has fortunately remained after it ceased to be a farm and is now used as an adventure centre.

Leave the track just beyond where it enters the farm

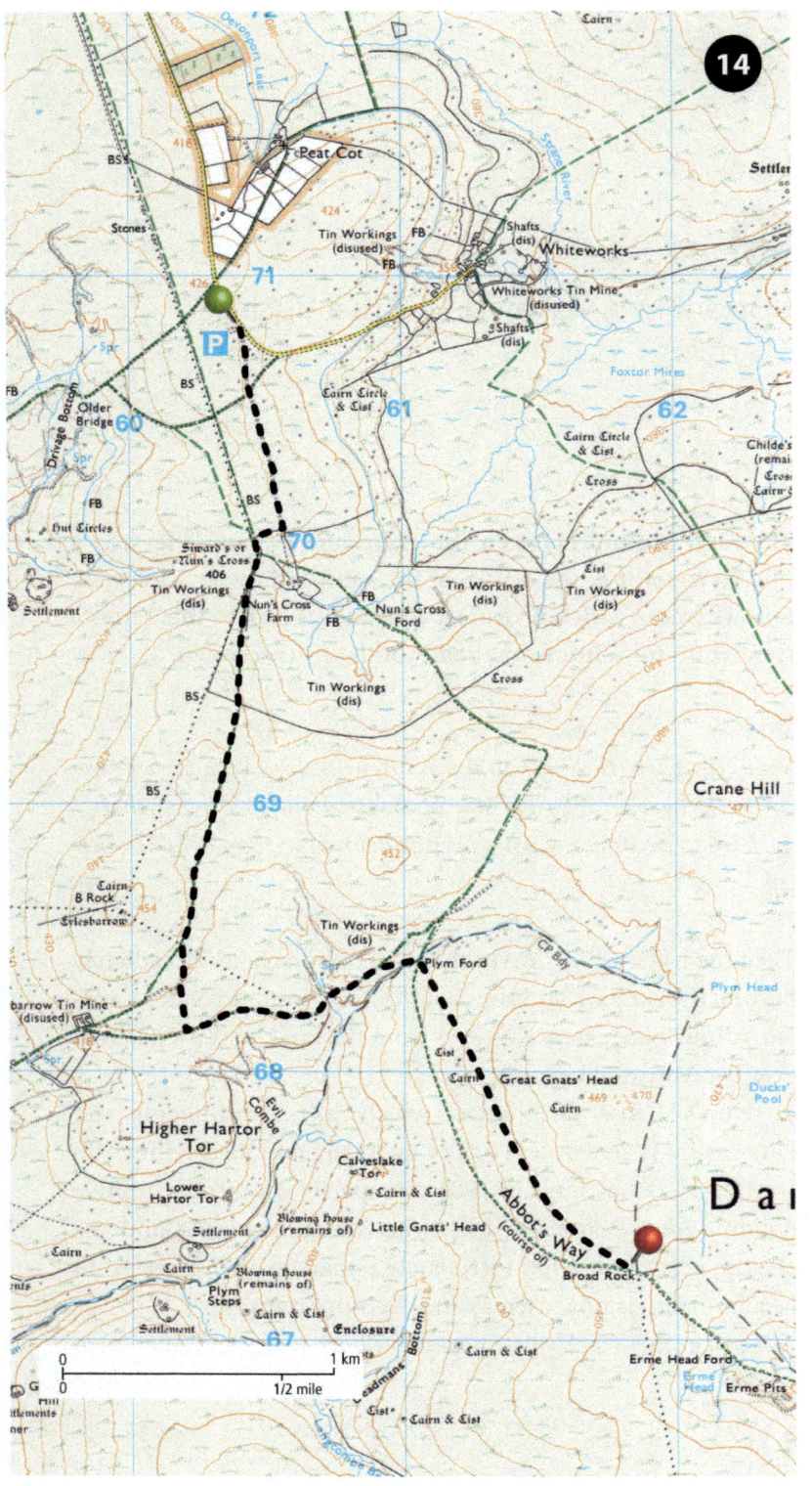

enclosures and proceed diagonally to the right to Nun's Cross (605699) which is now visible. This is visited on walk 12: see the description of that walk for details of its history.

The Tavistock branch of Jobber's Path is seen passing the cross and is now followed west of south. The track follows a prehistoric reave for the first 200 paces where there is one of the upright stones bearing the initials PCWW 1917 which mark the boundary of the catchment area of Burrator Reservoir. Here Jobber's Path and reave part company, the former branching to the left and the latter continuing up the hill ahead. Follow Jobber's Path, here a stony track which runs uphill to reach Eylesbarrow Common.

After about ½ mile a large mound comes into view, the track bending slightly to the left to avoid it. Another 300 paces on the track forks by a stone (602685) which Hemery (*Walking Dartmoor's Ancient Tracks*) has suggested may be a fallen guide stone. Take the left branch which leads to a junction with the Sheepstor – Plym Ford Mine track 601681). However the stony track terminates part way along this route and to continue follow a green path bending slightly to the right. If this path is missed the mine track will be met by continuing in a southerly direction.

Turn left into the mine track which is thus followed in an easterly direction. The valley of the Plym is seen below to the right and beyond it the hills of the centre of southern Dartmoor. The track descends and crosses a small stream, Crane Lake, by which are the ruins of a nineteenth century tin mine known as Wheal Katherine (607683). This was part of a huge mining operation centred on the Eylesbarrow area. The remains of the stamping mill which was used to break up the crude tin ore, with its wheel pit, can easily be made out. This is a pleasant sheltered spot and a good point for a rest before climbing on to the high moor.

Continue along the track for a further 300 paces to a point near some mounds and a stone wall, left, where a path branching to the right is entered, descending to the River Plym at Plym Ford (611684).

Looking across the river is seen a broad track ascending the hill beyond. Cross the river, which is normally relatively easy and follow the track which runs direct to Broad Rock over the high moorland between the valleys of the rivers Plym and Erme. The alignment of this track runs some distance to the left, ie north east, of that marked Abbot's Way on the OS map.

Looking to the right there are now extensive views of the valley of the Langcombe, a tributary of the Plym, the hills beyond and in the far distance, Plymouth Sound. A tributary of the Langcombe known by the rather unromantic name of Deadman's Bottom is crossed near its source. The track continues, ascending the hill beyond the stream and begins to descend into the Erme Valley leading to Broad Rock (61856724).

The rock, a natural one, is a flat boulder which lies among a number of smaller scattered rocks. Crossing gives the measurements as 11½ by 7½ feet. It bears the inscription BB, which stands for Blatchford Boundary and the words Broad Rock. It serves the dual purpose as marking the boundary of Blatchford Manor, Cornwood and the Dartmoor Forest. However recently most of the inscription has become covered with lichen growth.

Broad Rock, near the centre of the southern wilderness area, is one of Dartmoor's outstanding viewpoints. Ahead is the Erme Valley winding its way south through the hills from its source just below here, where the extensive tinners' workings known as Erme Pits are clearly visible. The spoil tips from the former Redlake clay works are seen just south of east and Western Whittabarrow, visited on walk 6, lies to the south south east.

Return by the same route.

Tunhill Rocks (walk 1) Peter Caton

Cist near Tunhill Rocks (walk 1) Michael Caton

Hut circle Grimspound (walk 2) MC

Ryders Hill (walk 3) PC

Huntngdon Warren (walk 4) PC

Huntingdon Clapper (walks 4 and 6) PC

OPPOSITE
Huntingdon Cross
(walks 4, 5 and 6)
PC

LEFT
Spurrell's Cross
(walk 7)
PC

BELOW
Three Barrows
(walk 7)
PC

RIGHT
Piles Copse
(walk 8)
PC

BELOW
Cist Near Piles
Copse (walk 8)
PC

Stone Circle Trowlesworthy (walk 9) PC

Ditsworthy Warren (walk 10) MC

Large cist Drizzlecombe (walks 10 and 11) MC

Menhir and Stone Row Drizzlecombe (walk 10) MC

Grim's Grave (walk 11) MC

Stone row and circle near Down Tor (walk 12) MC

Nun's Cross and farmhouse (walks 12 and 14) MC

Black Tor Falls (walk 13) PC

Blowing House Black Tor Falls (walk 13) PC

RIGHT
Broad Rock (walk 14) MC

Childe's Tomb (walk 15) PC

Waterfall East
Dart (walk 19) MC

LEFT
Duck's Pool
(walk 16) PC

Brown's House (walk 20) PC

Wistman's Wood (walk 21) PC

Rock basin, Great Mis Tor (walk 22) MC

Granite Setts Walkam Valley (walk 23) MC

Brat Tor (walk 24) PC

Black Tor
(walk 25)
PC

RIGHT
Steeperton Gorge
(walk 27)
PC

Teignhead Clapper
(walk 28)
PC

15

Fox Tor and Childe's Tomb – *4 miles*

This is a route to Fox Tor, along the hillside south of Fox Tor Mire, returning via Childe's Tomb.

Start
Whiteworks 2½ miles south of Princetown. There is parking space for a few cars 609708 near where the Devonport Leat crosses the road.

Whiteworks is a small settlement, still inhabited, which has its origin in the extensive tin mining carried out here in the nineteenth century. There is much evidence of the mining operations to the east of the parking area which can be reached by continuing along the road to its terminus past the inhabited houses, left.

To the south is the notorious Fox Tor Mire beyond which is seen Fox Tor, the objective of this walk. Under no circumstances try to make a direct line for the tor across the mire which can be dangerous. Cross the road and turn right along the path on the left side of the leat. This is followed, around the west side of the mire. There is a cist (608705) a short distance down the slope to the left of the leat just before the latter bends to the left.

The path is followed to just beyond a point near Nun's Cross Farm a short distance beyond where the leat bends to the right. Here is a track which crosses the leat by a clapper bridge.

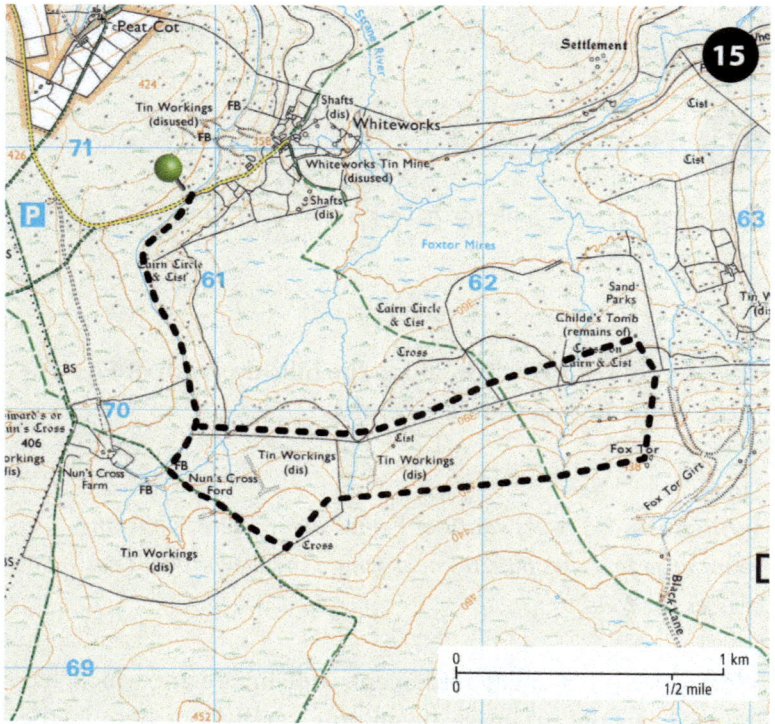

This is joined, turning left, descending to Nun's Cross Ford (609697) across the Nun's Cross Brook, a tributary of the River Swincombe which it joins after passing through Fox Tor Mire.

The next objective is a granite pillar (613695), marked cross on the OS map, about a third of a mile to the south east. A path leads to this which bends to the left on leaving the ford and passes through some tinners' workings (611696). However there are several paths in this area and it is easy to take the wrong one. Continue in the SW direction and the pillar, which is a prominent feature, comes into view.

It has been suggested that the pillar, known as Wheal Anne Cross is in fact the shaft of a cross of which the head is now missing, and there have been claims in the past to have found the head. It has an incised cross on its north western face.

The pillar is not associated with any ancient trackway but is a useful marker on the present route.

Turn left at the cross and follow a path which descends, passing an area of tinners' workings, to a gully through which runs the Whelam stream, a small feeder of the Swincombe. Walk a few yards to the left to locate the path across the stream (615696) which can be dry after periods without rain. From here the path continues diagonally up the hillside ahead. Follow this to a hill with some small rocks. This is Little Fox Tor. Walk to the right of this and continue along the path crossing another depression through which flows the infant T Gert stream. Cross this and continue direct to Fox Tor (626698) which is now in view.

Here is a good place to rest, take some refreshments and admire the fine views across Fox Tor Mire to the hills of Northern Dartmoor. It is believed to be the setting of Conan Doyle's Grimpen Mire in the *Hound of the Baskervilles*. To the right of the mire and half a mile in a direct line east of north of the tor, are the remains of Fox Tor Farm, a remote settlement built and abandoned in the nineteenth century. This features in Eden Philpot's novel *The American Prisoner*.

Fox Tor Mire was the proposed site for a reservoir in the 1970s which would have caused desecration of this fine area of moorland and severely damaged and reduced the extent of the southern Dartmoor wilderness. However through the determination and hard work of Lady Sylvia Sayer, patron of the Dartmoor Preservation Association and the support of many other objectors it was saved and is here today for all to admire, experience and enjoy.

The next objective is Childe's Tomb which lies near the edge of the mire and can be seen from the tor. To reach it descend the hillside, which has a lot of rock clitter, to a gateway in a stone wall. Pass through this; the tomb is then a short distance ahead.

Childe's Tomb was possibly originally a prehistoric cist on which, sometime in the Middle Ages, a cross was constructed. The original tomb was largely destroyed in the nineteenth century, the stones being used in the construction of the nearby Fox Tor Farm. It was later restored and now consists of a cist with a modern cross mounted on the capstone. The sides of the cist are of shaped stones which suggests they may be more recent in origin than prehistoric times. It lies on the Monk's Path and forms one of a long line of crosses to mark that route across the moor.

The well-known legend of Childe the Hunter is associated with it. Childe who, lost in a snowstorm killed, cut open and disembowled the carcase of his horse and crept inside in an attempt to keep warm. Unfortunately however he was frozen to death. He had stated in his will that his lands would now belong to the church where he was buried. With this prize in mind the Tavistock men set out to carry the body to the Abbey Church for interment there. However they were challenged by the people of Plymstock who assembled over the bridge of the Tavy with the intention of blocking the progress of the Tavistock men. The latter on hearing of this built another bridge across the river and carried home their prize in triumph.

The return route follows the stone wall to regain the Devonport Leat. Return to the wall, turn right and walk alongside it on the right, north side. This affords a relatively easy way and avoids some areas of rough ground in the area between the wall and Fox Tor Mire. It is necessary to cross the three streams seen at a higher level on the outward route; these can be negotiated quite easily. There is a cist (617699) near the other side of the wall just before reaching the Whelam stream. Also a few hundred yards east of north of this point is Goldsmith's

Cross, another of the crosses on the Monk's Path. This was named after Lt. Goldsmith R.N. in 1903 who discovered it lying on the ground. It was restored and set in a socket hole in a granite boulder.

The final section alongside the wall is a climb to join the leat. Here turn right to follow the outward route to the start.

16
Whiteworks to Duck's Pool – *7 miles*

Duck's Pool in the centre of the southern moor, like Cranmere Pool in the north, is a remote spot and objective for keen walkers looking for a challenge. This is probably the shortest and easiest approach with paths for virtually all of the route.

Start
As for walk 15 in the small car park at Whiteworks, south of Princetown.

The first section of this walk follows the route described for walk 15 alongside the Devonport Leat and then across the hillside south of Fox Tor Mire to Fox Tor. It is a good idea to pause here for a coffee or tea break before heading into the wild country ahead.

The way forward now requires careful identification as it is easy to mistake the route over the next few hundred yards. Walk round to the south side of the tor. To the south east, running up the hillside from left (east) to right (south), is seen a tinners' gully known as Fox Tor Gert, through which flows the Fox Tor stream. The gert leads to Black Lane, an ancient path which connects the Swincombe watershed with Wollake, a tributary of the River Erme. Be careful not to confuse the gert with another longer gully some distance beyond to the east, which is the upper part of the Swincombe valley running down from the river's source on Naker's Hill.

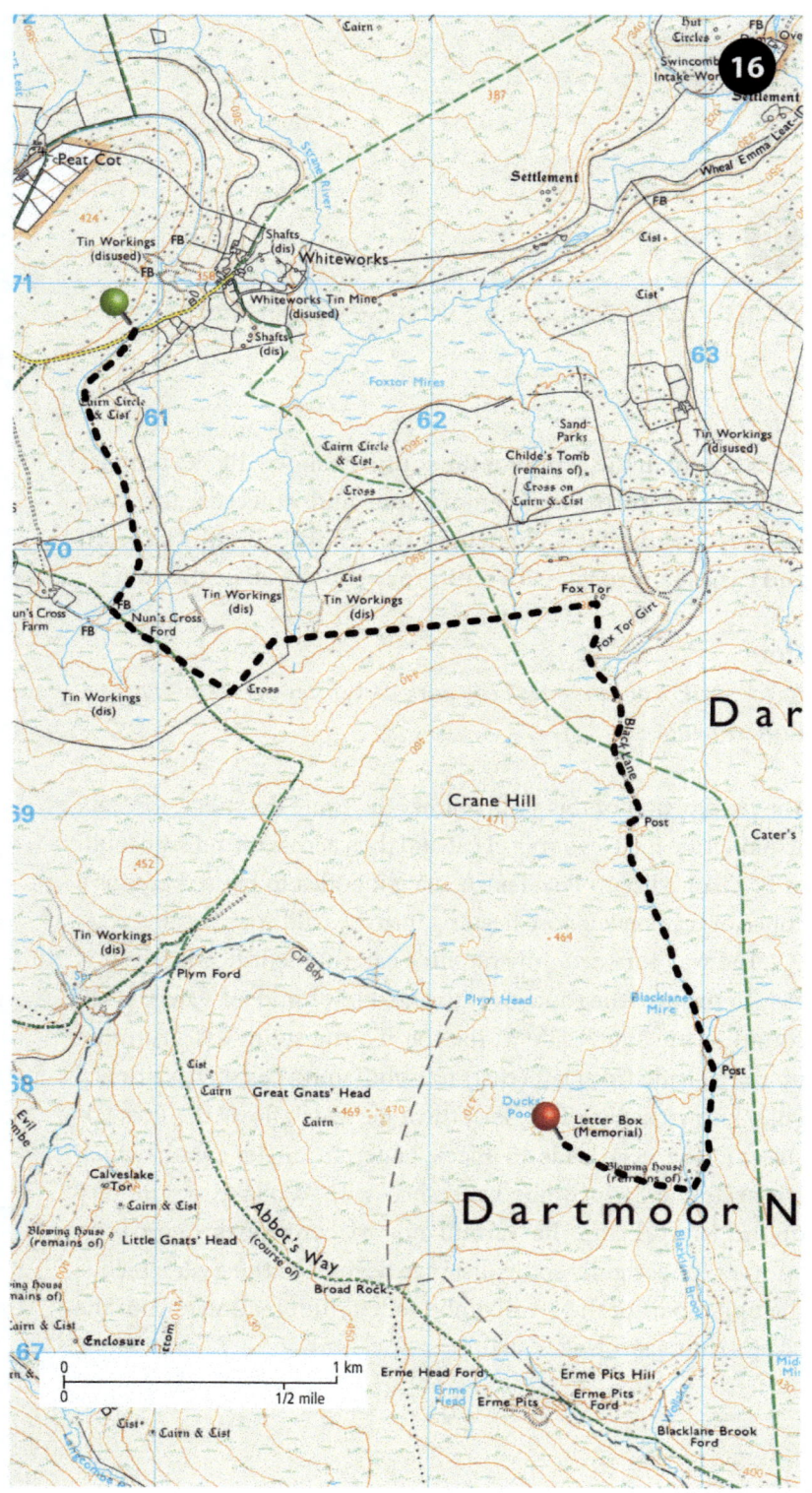

Make for a point on the gert (62646943) slightly east of south from the tor. A path leads from the tor in this direction; a short deviation to the right being required to avoid a branch of the gert, the source of a small tributary of the Fox Tor stream, where the ground is miry.

There is a tinners' blowing house here on the right. Ascend through the gert, walking on the right side where there is a reasonable path. A post, an upright much weathered railway sleeper, serving as a route marker comes into view approx. ½ mile from the tor. Here is the summit, beyond which the way descends into the watershed of the Erme.

The path turns sharp right (628690) and then, after a very short distance, left to resume the original direction. (Ignore a path which runs straight on at the latter point on to the slopes of Crane Hill.) The path now descends into the Wollake Valley, a tributary of the Erme. The ground is marshy in places but easily negotiated with care. As the descent continues the path improves. Another post is passed (631680), half a mile from the first one, near a small tributary, the Fishlake Gully, which enters the valley from the left.

Shortly beyond this a large area of rocks, tinners' mounds and walls opens up on the right. Continue downstream to meet a small tributary, the Duck's Pool stream. In the angle between this and the Wolake is another blowing house (630677).

Cross the Duck's Pool stream and turn right, walking now in a north westerly direction on firm ground where there are paths along the edge of the tinners' workings, to reach Duck's Pool (625678).

Don't be disappointed here, there is no water in it and there are no ducks! The so-called pool is merely a depression in the ground but to reach it gives a sense of adventure and achievement in this remote area. There is a letter box and a visitors book kept in a copper canister in a small cave beneath a large stone. The latter bears a memorial plaque to the great Dartmoor explorer William Crossing. Visitors are welcome to sign the book, stamp their postcards and leave them here for the next person to post.

It is possible to strike across the moor to take an alternative route back to the start but this is not recommended as the ground all around here is rough and much of it miry. It is best therefore to retrace the steps of the outward walk. This may be varied from Fox Tor to the start by following the route via Childe's Tomb described for walk 15.

Bellever Tor from Dunnabridge Pound – 3 miles

Bellever Tor is a prominent height towering above the forestry plantations south of Postbridge. It can be approached from the Postbridge National Park Centre by following the forestry paths but this is an alternative approach from the south through newtakes across open moorland.

Start
Dunnabridge Pound (645746) on the Dartmeet to Princetown road where there is parking space for several cars.

First visit Dunnabridge Pound on the northern side of the road. This was one of Dartmoor's two medieval drift pounds, the walls of which were built over a prehistoric structure. Horses and cattle grazing illegally in the east, south and west quarters of the moor were rounded up and collected in here, their owners having to pay a fine to reclaim them. Enter the pound through the gate by the roadside. On the left, built into the wall, is the so-called judge's chair, a stone bench. This intriguing structure, which has stone sides and roof, was the seat for the pound-keeper: it has been suggested that at one time it was the seat for stocks. The large slabs used to construct it are said to have been brought there from Crockern Tor, where they were used in medieval times for the tinners' parliament.

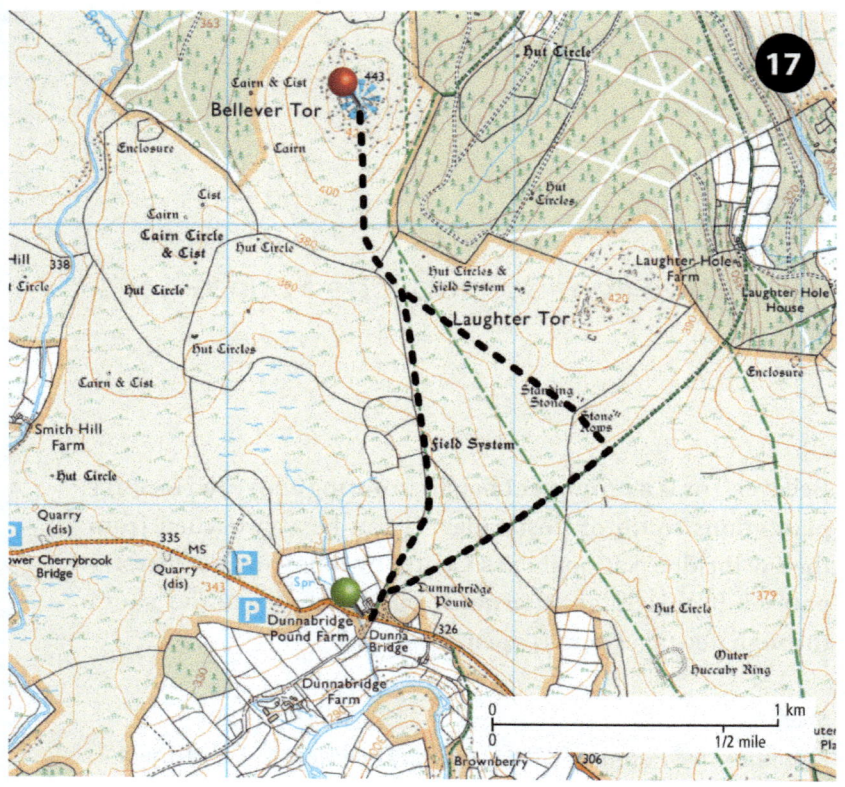

To start the walk pass through the gate to the left, north west of the pound and then, after 36 paces, branch left from the track, which runs to Bellever Hamlet on the East Dart, to take a direct route to Bellever Tor seen clearly ahead. The route, part of the Postbridge to Dunnabridge track which is marked on the OS map, initially follows a north east course to the corner of a newtake (647749). There is no obvious track over this section, but the general direction is easily found by noting the wall on the left which runs north and then east to this corner, where it assumes a northerly direction.

The route continues as a clear track running alongside the wall. It passes through a gate and continues to another gate which is below the tor. Just before reaching the latter gate the Huccaby to Bellever track is joined, right, this being followed on the return route. In the wall to the right of the gate are two unusual slotted gateposts. There are forestry plantations in the newtake to the right.

Pass through the gate and follow the track as it bends north to ascend the tor (644765). There are fine views of the surrounding moorland from the summit of this prominent height in the centre of Dartmoor.

For the return route walk back through the gate and diverge to the left along the Huccaby track. This follows a south east course and leads to the menhir known as Laughter Man (652654) seen on the left of the track just before reaching a wall. (This track should not be confused with the bridleway drawn as a straight line on the OS and British Mountain maps which does not appear to exist on the alignment shown.) Paths run from here to the summit of Laughter Tor, seen to the left. Pass through the gate; there is a double stone row to the left of the track, much robbed probably to build the newtake wall. Continue along the track to meet the Bellever-Huccaby Track, a short section of the north–south Track. Turn right into this to reach the start.

18

Along the East Dart from Postbridge – 4 miles

A dry leat which runs above the west side of the East Dart for some distance above Postbridge affords a useful path from which to explore this beautiful valley.

Start
Postbridge National Park Information Centre Car Park (647788).

Follow the well-trodden path branching north off the road to the west of the car park from which there is direct access to the left of the national park information centre. This is Drift Lane, an ancient route into the northern moor and part of the north-south track. It runs initially through a wide area between walls, known as a stroll, for ½ mile and enters the moor through a gate (643793). The way then continues alongside a newtake wall, right.

The East Dart lies below, right, beyond which is Hartland Tor. The imposing house seen across the river was built in the 1930s to replace an old farmhouse, once the home of the nineteen-century Dartmoor poet and newtake wall builder Jonas Coaker. The stone wall on the right is the upper side of a field which runs down to the river. Within this is a circular enclosure, known as Roundy Park, of prehistoric origin, stone walls having been built on the ancient ones in modern times.

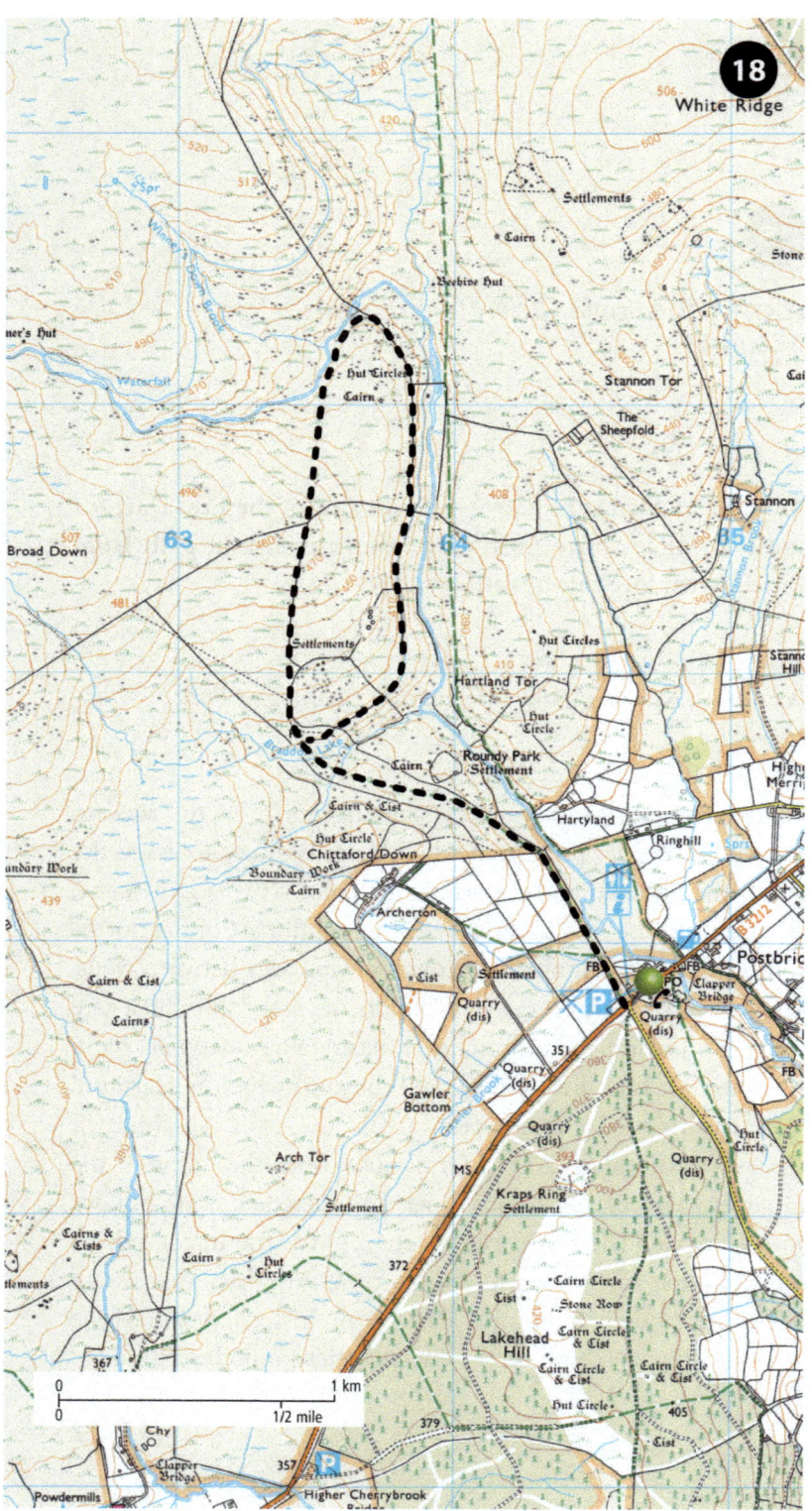

On the outside of this pound, adjacent to the north enclosure wall, is a large cist (639797), which is easily seen from the track. This is a fine monument with seven side slabs and two capstones. It can be visited by entering the enclosure through a gate (638796) seen on the right as the track descends to meet a stream, the Braddon Lake (636797).

The way passes between some bushes and meets the stream near where two channels join. Crossing the stream, which is normally straightforward with reasonable care, can best be accomplished by negotiating each channel just above the confluence.

Ascend the hill beyond to reach the bed of a dry leat (635797), making for a point just west, left, of a stile. The leat served the former gunpowder factory at Powder Mills, drawing its water from an intake of the East Dart.

Turn right here and follow the path which runs alongside the right side of the leat bed. This runs up the valley to near the former leat intake from the river. The path runs initially above the Braddon Lake valley, passing through the walls of the large pound known as Broadun. The leat bends to the left to take up a route high above the river. This is a spectacular walk through this deep valley. The going along the path is generally easy except for a short section where erosion has occurred which needs careful negotiation.

The leat is followed as far as a small clapper bridge (639812) where it bends right to take a course, to the intake. Leave the leat at this point and cross by the clapper beyond which the Dart follows a sharp hairpin bend to the left. There is a low hill ahead beyond which is seen Sittaford Tor just over a mile away. To continue up the valley follow a path which runs along the valley floor adjacent to the base of the hillside, left, thus avoiding a wide marshy area on the right between the path and the river. The path follows the valley, bending to the left, and approaches the river. There is a stile to cross (637813) and the way continues through some very picturesque river scenery. However beyond the stile the ground is uneven.

On approaching a wide marshy area leave the valley and ascend the hillside, left, in a slightly west of south direction. There is no path here but the going is fairly easy. A stone wall with a gate and nearby stile come into view. The walk here joins the return route of walk 19. Cross by the stile (635806) and follow the path downhill alongside a wall, passing through a gate in a wooden fence (634798) to return to the leat and the Braddon Lake crossing, retracing the outward route to the start.

19

Waterfall, East Dart – 3½ miles

This walk follows a route, on paths throughout, from Postbridge to Waterfall on the East Dart.

Start
Postbridge National Park Information Centre Car Park (647788).

The first part of the walk follows the route of walk 18 from Postbridge along Drift Lane to the moor gate (643793) and then alongside the wall on the right, to the Braddon Lake (636797) which is crossed just above the confluence of two channels. Climb up the hill beyond the stream to meet the bed of the dry Powdermills leat (see walk 18 for further details).

Cross the leat and continue left, westwards, along a path which runs alongside a stone wall. This forms the boundary of a prehistoric pound known as Broadun Ring on which modern walls have been built. It is a large enclosure and contains a considerable number of hut circles. The path soon bends to the right, following the wall northwards uphill. The way passes through a gate in a wooden fence.

Where the path forks (634799), near where the wall bends to the right and joins another wall, take the left branch and follow this uphill to a stile (632805) near the ridge summit. (The route from the leat to this fork follows a section of the return route of walk 18).

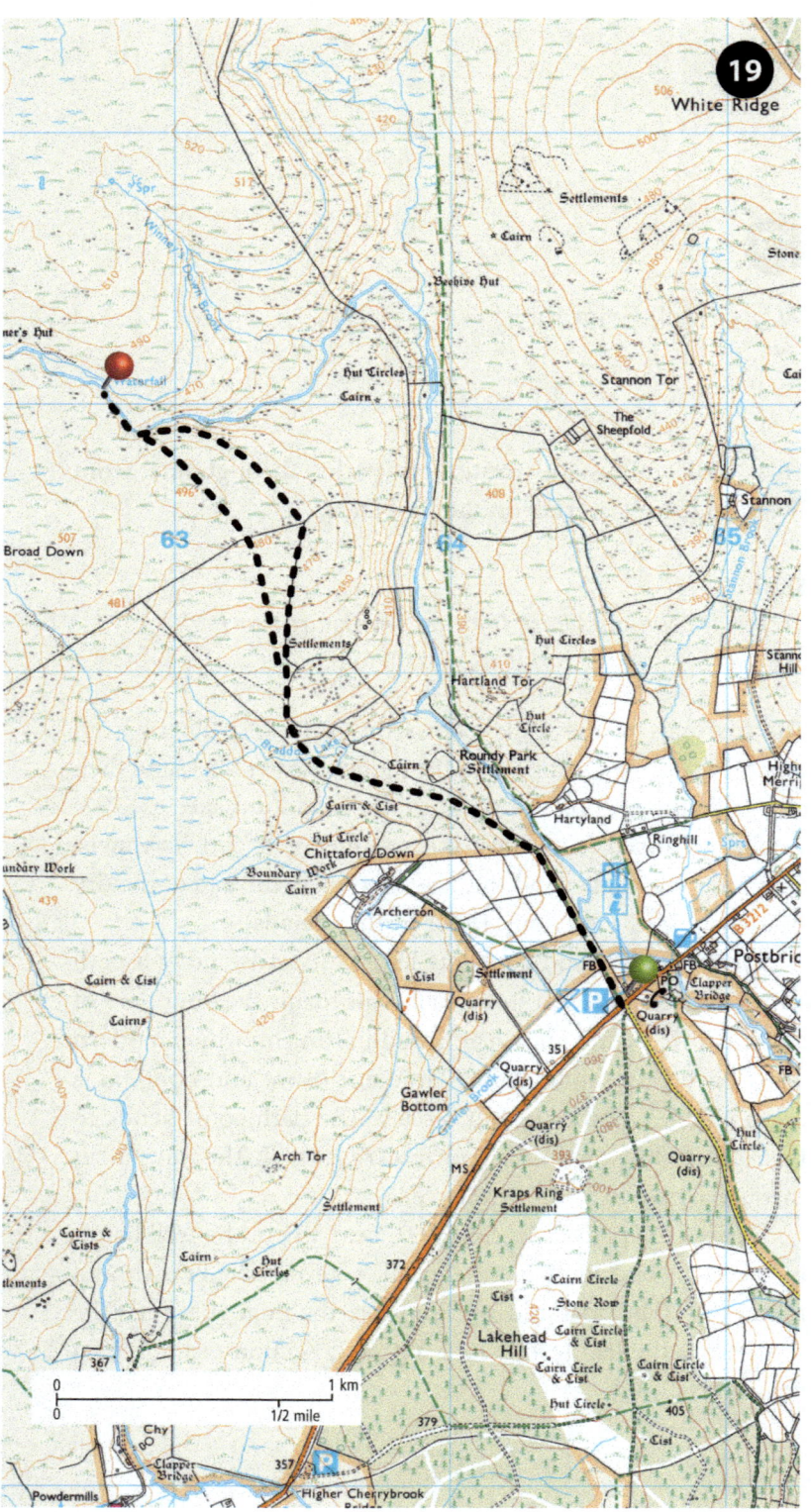

Cross here and continue ahead, passing to the left of a large rock, making for another rock directly ahead and ignoring a third one lying diagonally to the left. The East Dart Valley now comes into view beyond which is the wild country of northern Dartmoor. Diagonally to the left, about a mile away, the river runs through a deep canyon known as Sandy Hole Pass.

The way is then followed downhill in a north west direction to join the Dart at Waterfall (627811). Here the river runs over some large flat rocks before descending into a deep miniature gorge. This is a delightful spot to have a picnic or just sit and take in one of Dartmoor's gems. After rain the waterfall can be a most impressive sight.

The return may be made by the same route or by a slightly longer course to view more of this part of the Dart Valley. For the latter option re-enter the outward route and take a path which branches to the left (628809) just beyond a small streamlet which joins the Dart a short distance below Waterfall. This runs high above the impressive gorge through which the river flows and gradually bends uphill to the right, leading past a mound to a stile over a newtake wall (635806) near where two walls join. The path, which over the first section is stranded, is rather faint in places but is intact throughout. Ignore a branch which diverges to the left to take a course further along the valley. Cross the stile and take the path which runs downhill alongside a wall to meet the outward route. The route from the stile to the start follows the return route of walk 18.

20
Brown's House, West Dart – 6½ miles

This is a walk along the ridge of tors east of the West Dart, returning along the river valley.

Start
Two Bridges Car Park (609751). Should this be full an alternative small roadside parking area is available about 200 yards along the road in the Ashburton direction.

Pass through the gate north of the car park and follow the track, signed Wistman's Wood, leading to Crockern Farm, ½ mile. On reaching the latter take the path around the right of the farmhouse which leads to the open moor. A grassy path to Wistman's Wood branches off up the valley, left. Ignore this and continue along the path which bends to the right. After 80 paces this forks where the left branch is taken. After a further 80 paces this passes through a gateway and again forks. Then take the right branch which runs uphill for about two thirds of a mile to a ladder stile over a wall. Cross this to reach Littaford Tor (616768) the first of the tors which crown this ridge.

Continue on a path along the ridge to Longaford Tor (616779), a substantial pyramid-like outcrop which is well worth climbing for the splendid views of the West Dart Valley and way beyond. From here there is a path to Higher White Tor (620786) which is the next objective. There is a double stone row

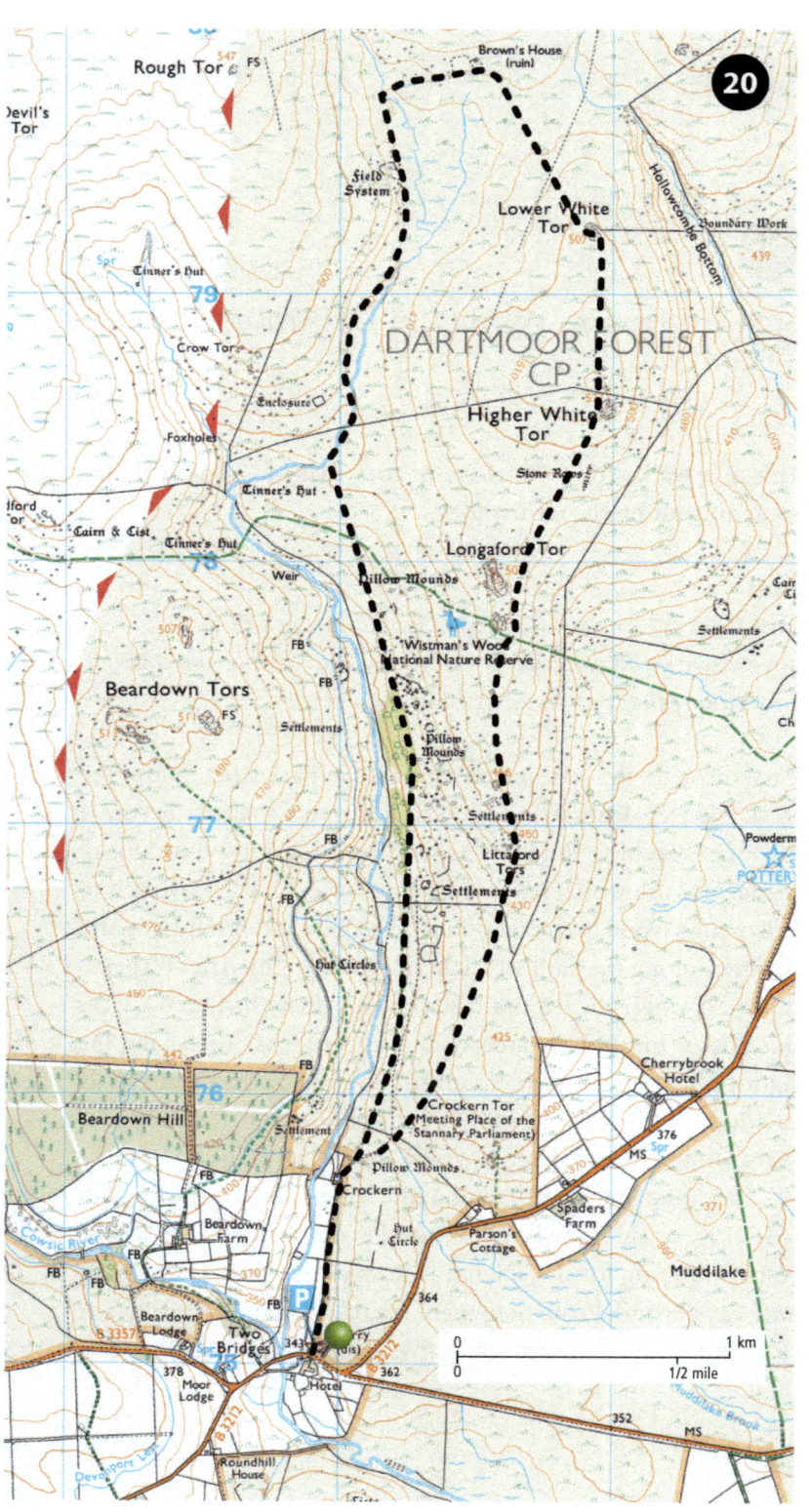

to the right on ascending towards the tor. This is a monument of only minor significance but worth a brief visit.

Higher White Tor is an ideal place for a rest and picnic before proceeding into wilder country. Brown's House is visible from here. Lower White Tor (619792) is the immediate objective which is reached by crossing the ladder stile on the north of Higher White Tor and following the path. This section can be boggy in a wet season but normally presents no problems. There is a lot of the white cotton grass on the approach to the tor which can be an attractive sight in summer.

The path becomes less clear at Lower White Tor but a small path runs round the left of the rocks. Ahead is Wildbanks Hill (not named on the OS map). Brown's House (615799) lies in the dip between there and Lower White Tor and is in a north of west direction from the latter from which two paths run downhill. Take the left branch which ends in a boggy area almost at the foot of the shallow valley about 400 yards from Brown's House. Some of the ground over this section is marshy and care, with appropriate detours, is required.

Brown's House, now a ruin, was a solitary dwelling in this remote spot believed to have been built early in the nineteenth century and long since abandoned. It is said that Brown had a pretty young wife of whom he was jealous and took her to live here to keep her from the eyes of other men. Baring-Gould in his book of Dartmoor published early in the twentieth century wrote:

> 'There are those still alive who remember when the chimney fell; and who had heard of both the building, the occupying, and the destruction of Browne's House. Few indeed have seen the ruin, for it is in so remote a spot that only the shepherd, the rush-cutter, and the occasional fisherman approach it.'

It can be said that this is still a lonely spot although today's visitor is more likely to meet a fellow rambler! (It should be mentioned that there is a ruined tinners' building in a marshy area at the bottom of the dip between Lower White Tor about 400 yards to the south of Brown's House. This must not be confused with the latter which is situated a short distance up the slope of Wildbanks Hill).

The return route follows the West Dart Valley. However much of the area on the Brown's House side of the river is mire and the west side is therefore followed. The river is conveniently crossed at a point (612797) between two 'kinks' in the river approximately south west of Brown's House. To reach this head in a line parallel with the stone wall of Brown's House. (There is no path over this section.) A triangular rock after about 100 yards acts as a useful guide. After crossing climb about 100 yards, turn left and follow the valley downwards, after a short distance passing above the head of a gully. The ground near the river is marshy but above this it is solid and grassy which, although there is no path, affords easy walking to a point where the river makes a right angle bend to the right. There is a very short rocky section just before the latter point is reached which is easily negotiated.

The river is re-crossed here (610785). This can easily be done, with care, as there are some large rocks in the riverbed which are well placed for stepping across. The crossing place is just upstream from where a wall crosses the river; Longaford Tor is seen diagonally to the left. Immediately after making the crossing pass over the wall by a ladder stile.

The next objective is Wistman's Wood, one of Dartmoor's three ancient oak woods. This is ½ mile away in a south east of south direction. The ground over this section is rather rough but paths are available to assist the walker. A course I have found useful is to turn right and follow the river downstream by 330 paces along a path by the river, to a point (609783) just downstream from a ladder stile over a wall on the opposite bank. Here by a large rock a path branches at right angles to the left and this is followed uphill. When it divides take the right fork and further on take another right fork to lead straight to some clitter near the wood, which is easily negotiated.

The final section of the walk is also followed in walk 21; see the description of this for further details.

Follow the path which runs above the wood and then down the valley to join the outward route near Crockern Farm. The path crosses a wall by a stile not far from Wistman's Wood and another stile after a further ½ mile.

21
Devonport Leat and Wistman's Wood – 4 miles

The footpath alongside the upper part of the Devonport leat affords a useful route along the West Dart valley from Two Bridges to the riverside opposite Wistman's Wood, one of Dartmoor's three ancient oak woods. The river is then crossed to visit the wood and join the return route of walk 20.

Start
Two Bridges Car Park (609751). If this is full park in a small roadside area 200 yards along the road in the Ashburton direction.

From the car park walk westward along the road towards Princetown, for a short distance, crossing the West Dart and then, after 80 paces, take a path which leaves the road, right. This is rough in places with high steps and should be negotiated with care. The path leads past a deep wooded dell, right, through which the River Cowsic flows just above its confluence with the West Dart. There are several waterfalls and this is a most attractive approach to the moor. A footbridge and stiles are crossed and the path then joins a track which runs from the Tavistock road west of Two Bridges to Beardown Farm and beyond.

Follow this, turning right, and cross the Cowsic by a stone bridge. After a short distance, Beardown Clapper Bridge over

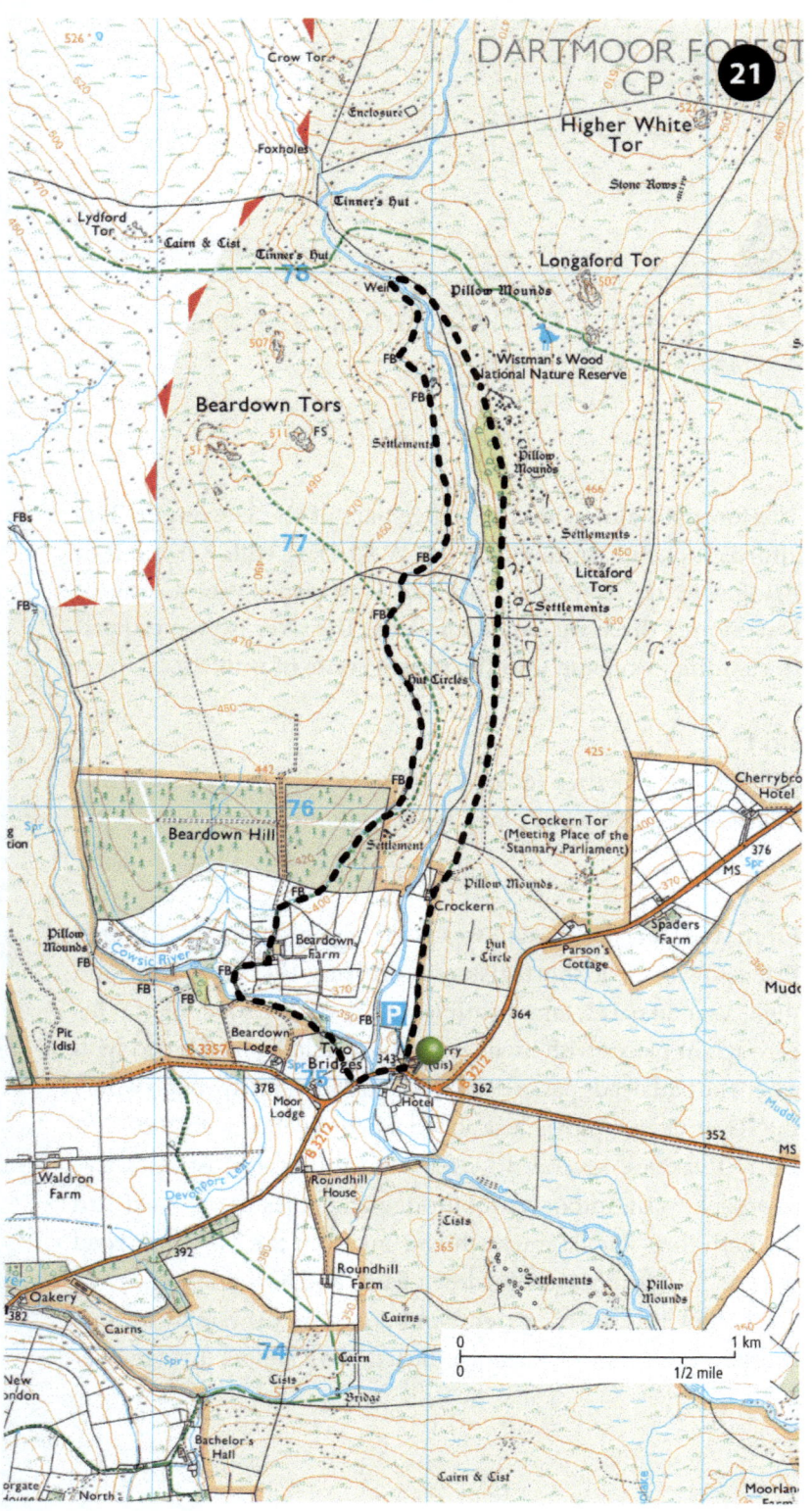

the Cowsic is seen across a field to the left. This rather fragile structure is made up of a number of small stone sections, rather than the usual large slabs and on several occasions has been damaged during periods of floods.

Do not take the path across the clapper but continue along the track, passing the entrance to the farm, right, then bending to the left to reach a bridge over the Devonport Leat (604756). Leave the track here and turn right, following the path along the right bank of the leat. The latter is followed through a forestry plantation, crossing several stiles, to emerge on to the open moor (608760) above the West Dart. Here is a place to pause and take in the spectacular views across the deep valley.

Continue along the leat path as it follows the contours above the river for 1½ miles to the leat inlet weir (609780). Wistman's Wood, with Littaford and Longaford Tors on the ridge above, are seen on the far side of the river.

The West Dart can be crossed either at the weir if the river level is relatively low, when only the central of three channels has water in it, or about 30 yards downstream just above the weir where there are some rocks. The ancient Lych Way, along which the dead were carried across the moor for burial at Lydford Churchyard, crossed the river near here, although there is no visible track on this part of it. Further up the valley Crow Tor, an unusually shaped rock, is seen perched on a hill beyond where the Dart makes a double bend.

There is a wooden stile over a wall close to the weir. Cross over this and take a rough path running to the right at an approximately 45 degree angle from the wall, heading in a direct line to Longaford Tor. Some of this section is boggy and suitable deviations may be necessary. On meeting a path running parallel to the river turn right and follow the return route of walk 20.

The route runs parallel to the river, passing above the wood which is a national nature reserve. Note the stunted oak trees with various mosses and lichens growing in the branches. This is a romantic place and has been the inspiration of many artists and poets. It has been suggested that the name Wistman's is derived from the dialect word 'wisht' meaning eerie/uncanny.

There are numerous hut circles to the left of the path and some buries built for Wistman's Warren which was situated near the upper end of the wood. The warren house, unlike others on the moor which were made of stone, was a wooden building and interestingly the warrener is the major character in Eden Phillpot's novel *The River*.

The path continues south beyond the wood and after a short distance crosses a stile over a wall. Pass over this and after ½ mile, over another stile making for Crockern Farm ahead. The route here joins a track which passes to the left of the farm and then follows the farm track leading back to the start.

22
Great Mis Tor and Merrivale – 3 miles

This is a walk to the fine viewpoint of Great Mis Tor with an extension to the Merrivale Bronze Age antiquities.

Start
Four Winds Car Park (561749) on the Princetown to Tavistock Road.

The car park is on the site of the former Foggintor School which served the children of workers in the granite quarries nearby from 1915 until 1936.

Looking north, across the road, is the lofty Great Mis Tor which is the first objective of the walk. There is a track over the route which leaves the road opposite the right side of the car park. Follow this which runs for a short distance in a slightly west of north direction and then bends towards the north east. After just over half a mile it turns to the left to assume a northerly direction and leads to a small outcrop known as Little Mis Tor which consists of three rock piles.

There are fine views to the left across the Walkham Valley to Staple and Roos Tors. The OS map shows the track as terminating just beyond Little Mis Tor but it does continue, partly as a grassy way, to the rocks below Great Mis Tor. Follow this; on the left as the tor is approached, is a tall boundary stone.

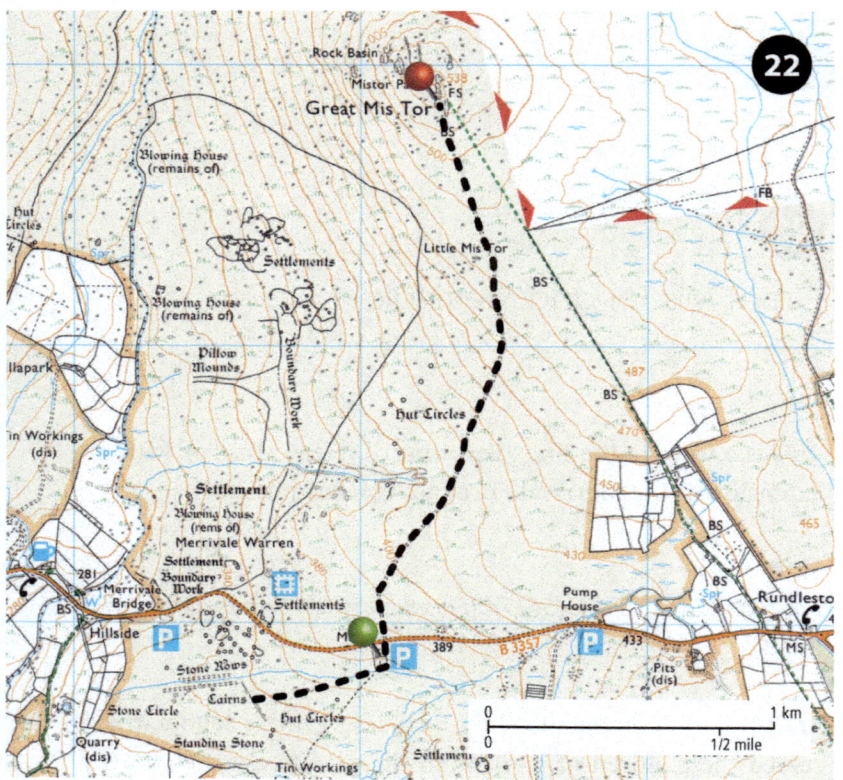

It is worth spending some time exploring the tor. Walk around it and admire the views which extend over much of Dartmoor, including Great Links Tor, Fur Tor, High Willhays and Cut Hill in the north and the southern heights of Hay Tor, Saddle Tor and Rippon Tor. To the south east, way beyond the moor, are seen the Tamar and Tavy valleys.

On the top of the north side of the large rock forming the centre of the tor is a fine rock basin known as Mistor Pan. When filled with water this is an attractive sight. To find it climb the rock, with care, from the north side.

Return by the same route.

The walk may be extended by a visit to the Merrivale prehistoric antiquities which are ½ mile slightly south west of west of the car park. These rank with those at Drizzlecombe as the finest complex of Bronze Age monuments on the moor. There are four stone rows, two cists, a menhir, a stone circle and several cairns. Two of the stone rows are double and run almost parallel to each other. The southern row has a cist inserted within it near the centre of the row, a most unusual feature. South of this row is a large cist with the capstone in position but split across the centre where a piece of it was cut out to make gateposts. The third, shorter single row runs at an angle south west of the second row. Further south is the stone circle, made of small stones, and the large menhir. Near to the latter are a few stones of the fourth row.

A reave runs south east from the south ends of the double rows. Beyond this is a line of guide posts bearing the letters T and A Tavistock and Ashburton marking the old track that connected these places across the moor. To the north of the rows is a group of hut circles among which is an abandoned stone apple crusher known as the plague market. Food was left there for collection by those stricken with that horrible disease.

Return by the same route.

23

The Walkham Valley – *5 miles*

Leats on the west side of the Walkham Valley afford a convenient route to the Langstone prehistoric settlement and stone circle.

The walk passes through the Merrivale firing range.

Start
Merrivale on the Princetown to Tavistock road. Car parking is available by the old bridge over the river Walkham (550751); there is also space for two or three cars at the side of the quarry track (see below) which is nearer the start of the walk.

From the old bridge walk past the Dartmoor Inn and follow the road towards Tavistock, passing the now disused quarries and associated buildings, right. A short distance beyond the last building, a white house, a track which served the quarries diverges to the right. This is entered and followed for 20 paces to a footpath which branches to the left just before reaching the concrete base of a former building. Follow the path to a concrete hut surrounded by a stone wall which is passed on the left. Continue up the hill for 20 paces to reach the dry bed of the long abandoned Longford Leat (545752). The leat, which is shown on the OS maps, is rather overgrown near the point of entry but there should be no difficulty in locating it.

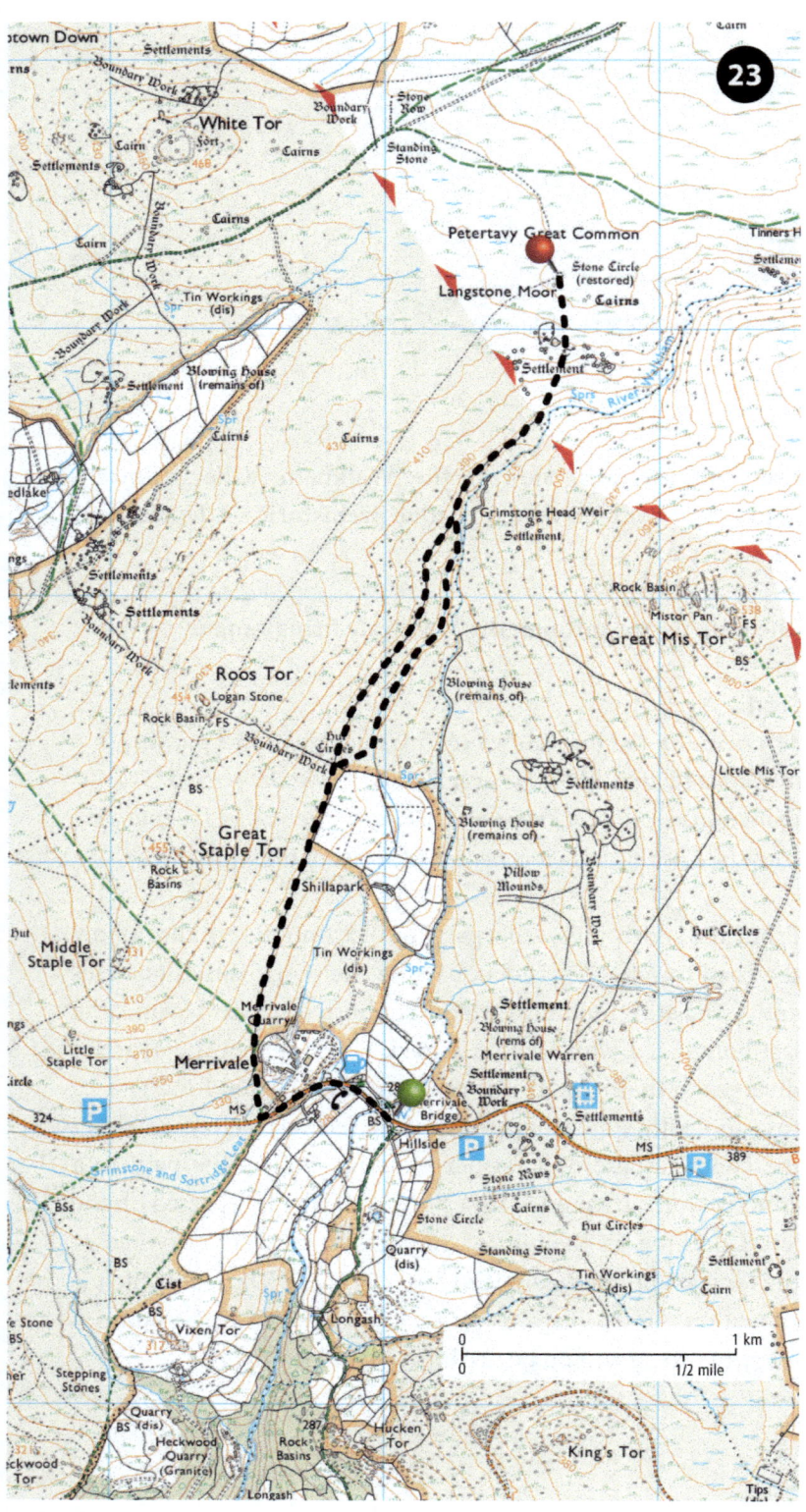

The leat is now followed along its course east of north. Some sett makers bankers are passed left. These were used as open-air benches on which granite setts were cut for roads and pavements. A large amount of granite was taken from this area over the centuries and this was developed commercially in the latter part of the nineteenth century (see Simon Dell and John Bright *Dartmoor's Sett Makers*).

Great Staple Tor with its rock piles is seen above on the left, and to the right, above the east side of the river valley, is Great Mis Tor. After ½ mile the leat passes the north west corner of the Shillapark Farm enclosures (547761) and continues alongside the north west wall. It then runs across the open moor to the former intake on the river. This may be followed but an attractive alternative is to descend towards the river to the still functioning Grimstone and Sortridge Leat, now seen below as it emerges from its course through the farm enclosures and to follow this to its intake at 553773. This leat was cut to provide a water supply for houses and farms in the Dartmoor border country. About fifty paces from its emergence from the farm enclosures it is crossed by a single span clapper bridge. This is a convenient point to descend to the river to view the upper Merrivale blowing house (552766). This was excavated in recent years.

If this detour is made return to the clapper to recross the leat which is too wide to step across with ease. Continue up the valley alongside the leat. As the Grimstone Leat intake point is approached; the dry Longford Leat is seen running above the river ahead. Climb the hillside to rejoin this and continue to its former intake (556777).

Continue to the Langstone prehistoric settlement which is on the hillside a few hundred yards north of here. This little known site, which consists of six whole or partial enclosures and 51 hut circles, is well worth exploring. The largest, uppermost enclosure is the most complete. To find the Langstone circle (556782) walk a short distance east of north from here. The circle was badly damaged by military firing during the Second World War. Some of the stones were broken and others overturned. It is a rather sad site but hopefully one day it will be restored as far as possible, although that would be far from easy.

The return route may be made along the Longford leat which is very useful in affording an easy course through an area of clitter below Roos Tor.

24
Upper Rattlebrook Valley – 6 *miles*

Following an old peat track from near the Dartmoor Inn, Lydford to the Rattlebrook valley, returning along the route of the former Rattlebrook Railway provides a circular walk through the spectacular scenery of north east Dartmoor.

Start
Car park (526853) reached by driving along the short track which diverges from the road immediately to the north of the Dartmoor Inn, Lydford.

Follow the track that goes east, into the moor, from the left, north east corner of the car park. This runs alongside a wall, left and after ½ mile reaches the River Lyd. Cross this either by the large stepping stones or the footbridge.

Two tors are seen on the ridge ahead, Arms Tor to the left and Brat Tor to the right. On the latter is Widgery Cross, set up in 1887 by the Dartmoor artist William Widgery to commemorate Queen Victoria's golden jubilee. This is a large cross and differs from others on Dartmoor in that it is built up from blocks of stone rather than being cut from a single piece. The walk now follows the track which ascends the ridge to a point midway between these tors. This first runs diagonally to the left and then, about half way up the ridge, bends to the right. The way is wide and easy walking initially, but on the second half of the ascent

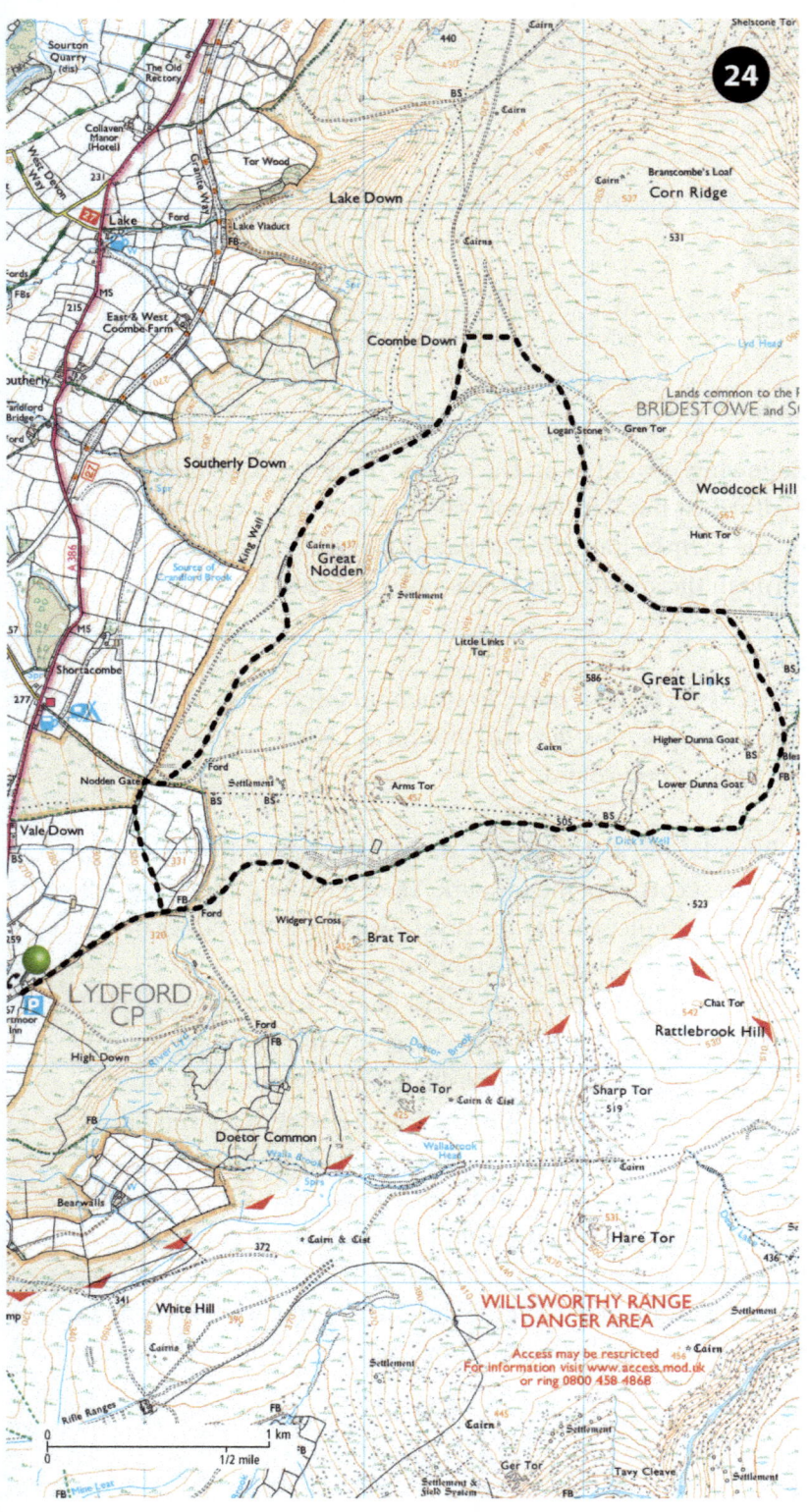

there are some marshy areas which require walking on suitable firm ground alongside the track. Some tinners' workings are to be seen to the left of the upper part of the track.

Near the top of the climb, about midway between the two tors, the way crosses a path (542860). Looking back from here are distant views into Cornwall. Continue along the track, diagonally right; two further tors are to be seen. After about ½ mile from the top of the ridge the extensive tinners' workings at the head of the Doe Tor Brook are passed, right and to the left is the hill crowned by Great Links Tor, although much of the tor is not visible from this point. The track descends to cross tinners' workings (552861) where there is a boundary stone, left bearing the letters BS and L, signifying Bridestowe and Sourton, and Lydford, being at the intersection of the boundaries of these two parishes.

The way continues uphill, alongside a gully on the right. Lower Dunnagoat Tor comes into view left and in the distance, diagonally right is seen Fur Tor, the most remote on Dartmoor. The track then descends into the Rattlebrook valley and enters an area of tinners' mounds where it turns left to run to the right of Lower Dunnagoat Tor. A ruined building is seen in the valley below; this is Bleak House, the former residence of the Manager of the Rattlebrook works. Above this is Green Tor.

Continuing in what is now an east of north direction the Rattlebrook railway embankment is seen ahead. The mine track descends to cross the stream north of Bleak House; this is ignored and a track running west of north taken to join the rail track. Along this section the remains of various buildings associated with the peat works are seen to the right. The track is in rather poor condition as it approaches the railway, which is joined at a point (556871) a short distance from where the latter ran through a cutting. Hunt Tor is seen ahead and Kitty Tor to the right beyond the Rattlebrook Peat Works which the railway served.

The railway was opened in 1879 to carry peat from the works to the main railway line at Bridestowe. Initially horse worked and later powered by a petrol engine it closed in the 1930s

Turn left and follow the railway formation, passing through the cutting. Great Links Tor is now a prominent feature on the left. The track bends to the right and assumes a north westerly direction for some distance. Gren Tor is seen on the right and the rounded hill of Great Nodden lies below, left. The track continues, crossing the River Lyd near its source, to the spot known in the days of the Railway as points, where the trains used to reverse and assume a south westerly direction to enable them to negotiate the considerable gradients. A green track which leaves the railway at 547884 and rejoins it at 545884 affords a short cut across the loop.

Continue along the rail track as it runs to the right, west, of Great Nodden. There are more fine views from here into Cornwall. The line ran over an embankment for a short section; this may be followed but it is easier here to walk along a track, part of the King Way, the old road from Tavistock to Okehampton which here runs parallel to it on the left. The rail route is then rejoined at the end of this section. It runs through a deep cutting and re-emerges into the Lyd Valley, high above the river and on to near Nodden Gate where a track from Fox and Hounds Cross to a ford across the river is met. The railway route is left behind at a point where it bends, right into a cutting from where a track leads on for a short distance to join the Noddon Gate track at 530863. Turn right here and walk the few yards to the gate; a mound is passed, right. Pass through the gate and note the boundary stone on the left of it on which are inscribed the letters B for Bridestowe and L for Lydford.

This is now less than ½ mile from the outward route which is rejoined by following a right of way across a large field to join the track to the car park west of the footbridge over the river.

Enter a gate adjacent to the left of Noddon Gate, turn right and follow a path which runs alongside a stone wall. This is another section of the King Way. Although this leads to near the car park it runs through private land which is avoided by turning left at a point approx. 160 paces from the gate where there is an interesting stone stile over the wall on the right. From here pass through a gate and walk diagonally up the hill when a ladder stile comes into view which is crossed to join the outward path.

25

Black Tor, West Okement Valley – *4 miles*

The West Okement in north east Dartmoor runs through some of Dartmoor's wildest and most majestic scenery. This walk follows a track to Black Tor, a fine viewpoint on the east side of the valley.

Start
Car park at Meldon (562917).

Walk through the gate out of the car park and turn left to take the track to the Meldon reservoir dam, passing through another gate. Cross the dam, noting the deep gorge to the left. This is part of Meldon Gorge, the remainder of which lies beneath the waters of the reservoir, right.

Turn right to follow the path round the eastern side of the reservoir to a point (562913) where a track is seen branching to the left. Follow this which runs diagonally up Longstone Hill in an east of north direction, almost doubling back on itself. After ½ mile the track bends to the right to run south. Prior to the bend it divides into two alignments, the left being the main one. The two tracks run parallel and rejoin after the southerly direction has been attained. Views of the West Okement Valley open up and on the left is the deep valley of the Red-a-ven, a West Okement tributary.

The track soon divides again, when the right branch is taken.

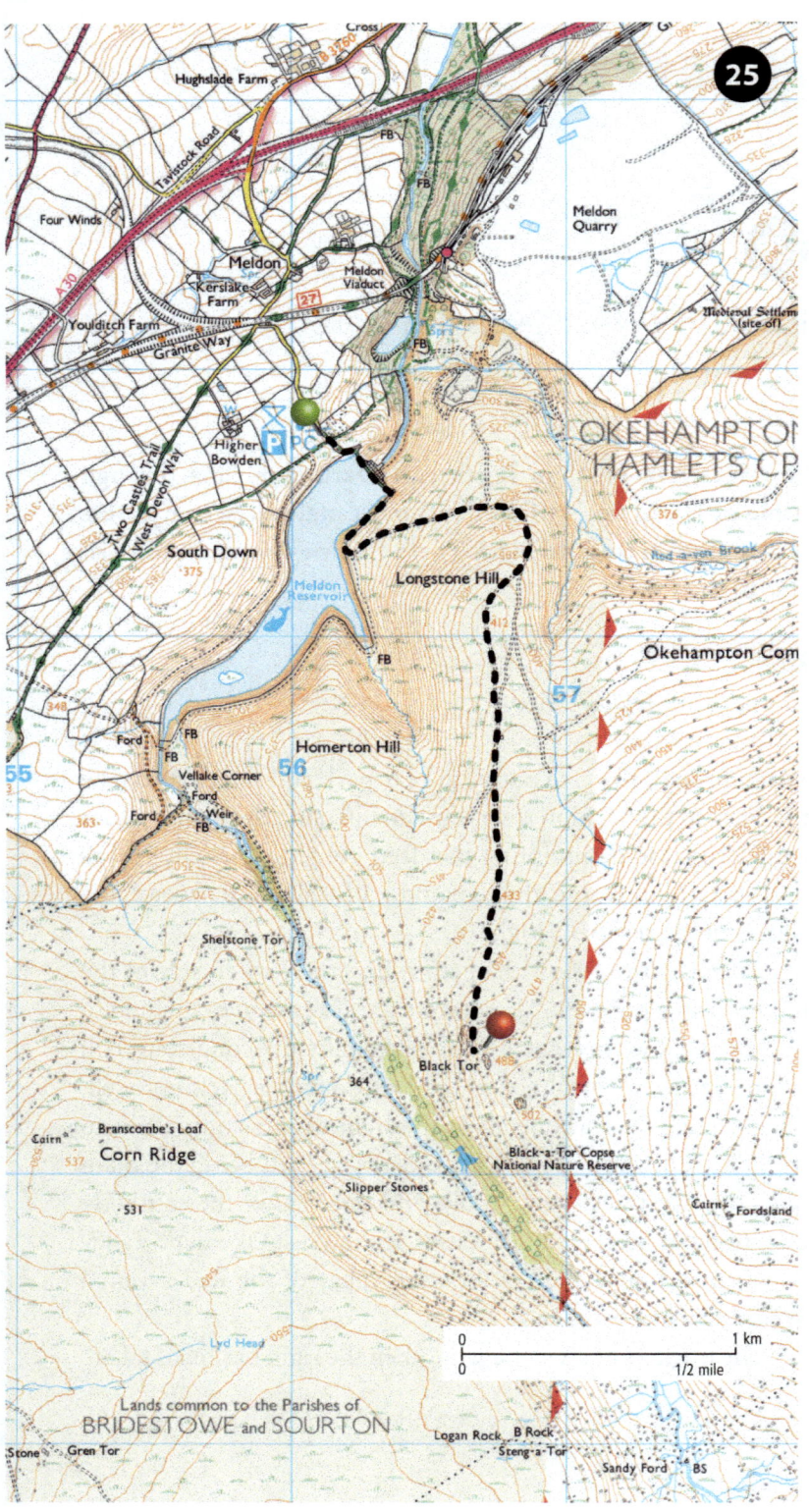

Continue to where the track ends just short of Black Tor. The route is easy to follow. It crosses a green area where the track is unclear and is rather rocky as the tor is approached, but this presents no significant problems.

Walk on to the tor and take in the fine view of this beautiful valley. Below the tor and beside the river is Black Tor Copse, one of Dartmoor's three ancient oak woods. This can be visited by walking down to the river from the tor. Like the other two woods, Wistman's Wood (walks 20 and 21) and Piles Copse (walk 8) this is an enchanting place and well worth a visit.

Return by the same route.

26

Yes Tor and High Willhays – *7 miles*

This is a route from Moor Gate above Okehampton to the summit of Dartmoor's highest hills – Yes Tor and High Willhays.

The walk enters the Okehampton firing range.

Start
Car Park at Moor Gate (591932).

From the car park walk across the cattle grid to enter the moor. Three tors are seen ahead: left to right these are Rowtor, West Mill Tor and Yes Tor. A road is seen ahead, running in a south east direction which crosses a stream, the Moor Brook. Ignore this and turn right to follow a road which runs alongside a wall, right. After ½ mile this gradually bends left, and runs along the left bank of the Moor Brook. Ignore tracks which branch to the right and left along this section.

Although made into a tarmac road for military purposes, this is in fact an ancient route to Dinger Tor above the West Okement Valley, which according to Hemery, forms part of Dartmoor's north–south path. It leads right across the northern moor via Postbridge and then over the southern moor to Harford Moor Gate near Ivybridge (walk 8). It is followed as it ascends the col between Rowtor and West Mill Tor where the

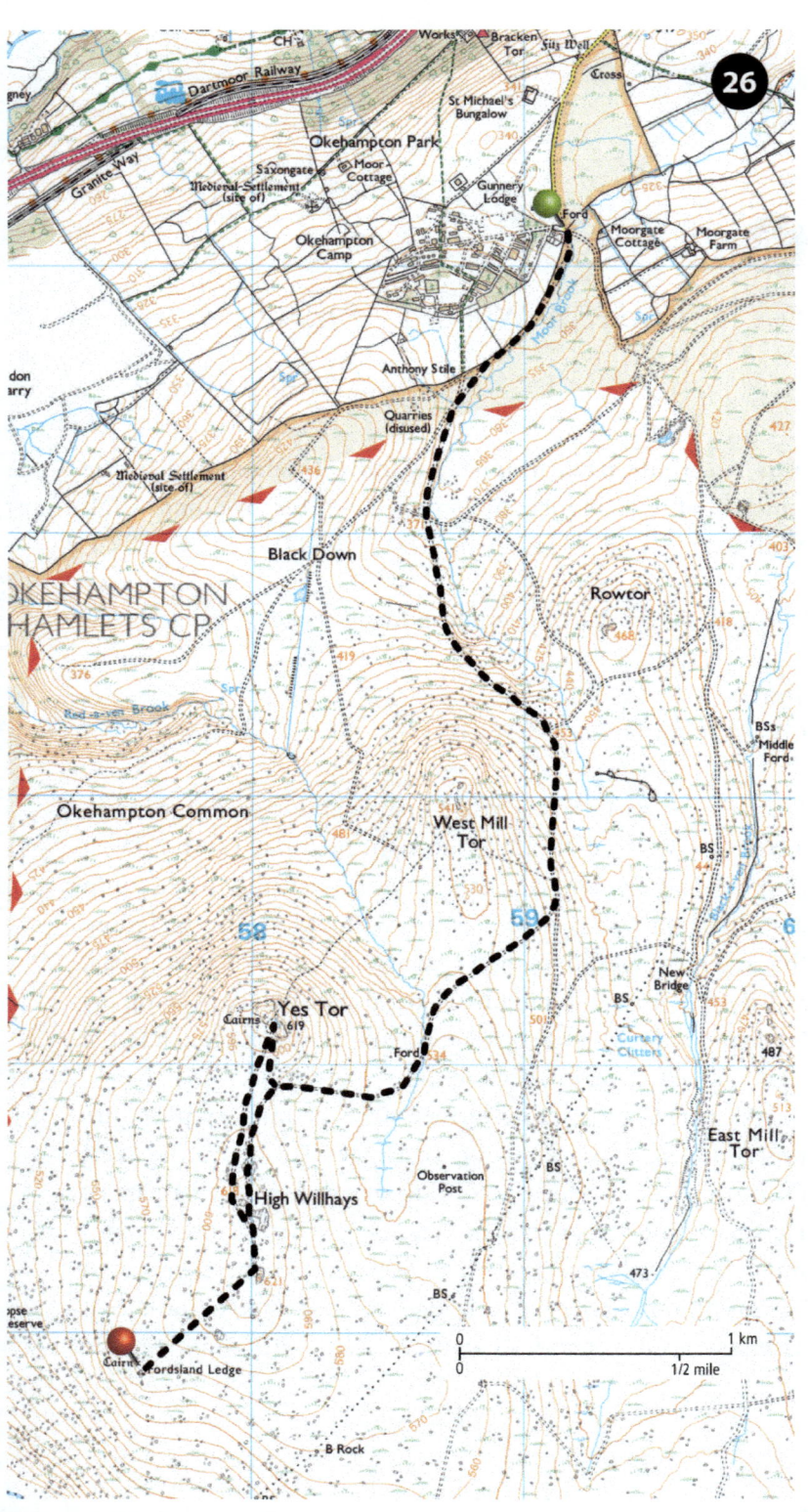

tarmac surface ends. Continue to a point where a track to Yes Tor and High Willhays diverges to the right (591906). Follow this, which runs in a south west direction to cross the Red-a-ven Brook near its source, before ascending to reach the col between these two heights.

It is worth climbing each of these as the views are different. Turn right to reach the summit of Yes Tor. From here are superb views not only of Dartmoor but for many miles beyond into central and north Devon including, on a clear day, Exmoor and the Bristol Channel. North east Cornwall can also be seen.

To reach High Willhays follow a track which runs south along the ridge. High Willhays, 12 feet higher than Yes Tor, is both the highest point on Dartmoor and in England south of Ingleborough in Yorkshire. From here much of Northern Dartmoor is in view including the central areas around Cranmere Pool.

A third point worthy of a visit is Fordsland Ledge, a small pile of rocks reached by taking a path which descends 200 feet in a south west direction from High Willhays. From here there are splendid views of the West Okement Valley.

Return to High Willhays and then follow a track which runs parallel to the outward route to rejoin the latter below Yes Tor.

27
Steeperton Gorge – 7 miles

On its descent from the high moor, the River Taw passes through a gorge which is one of the most spectacular features of the northern moor. This walk approaches the gorge from Belstone via a track to a former tin mine known as Knack Mine, returning along the Taw Valley.

The walk passes through part of the Okehampton firing range.

Start
Belstone where there is a car park in the village.

From the car park walk into the village centre, noting the stocks on the left of the green. Also on the left is Belstone Pound, once used to contain stray farm animals and now a small garden. Then take the right fork and when the road divides again continue straight ahead along a no through road which leads uphill to the moor gate (616933).

Pass through the gate and follow the track which leads to Culliver Steps on the East Okement River. This runs straight alongside a wall, right and soon bends gradually to the left, around Watchet Hill. The Knack Mine track branches off to the left at 613930, a few paces after the wall has turned sharp right. Take care to avoid grassy tracks which also branch off to the left. Continue along the mine track which runs in an approximately

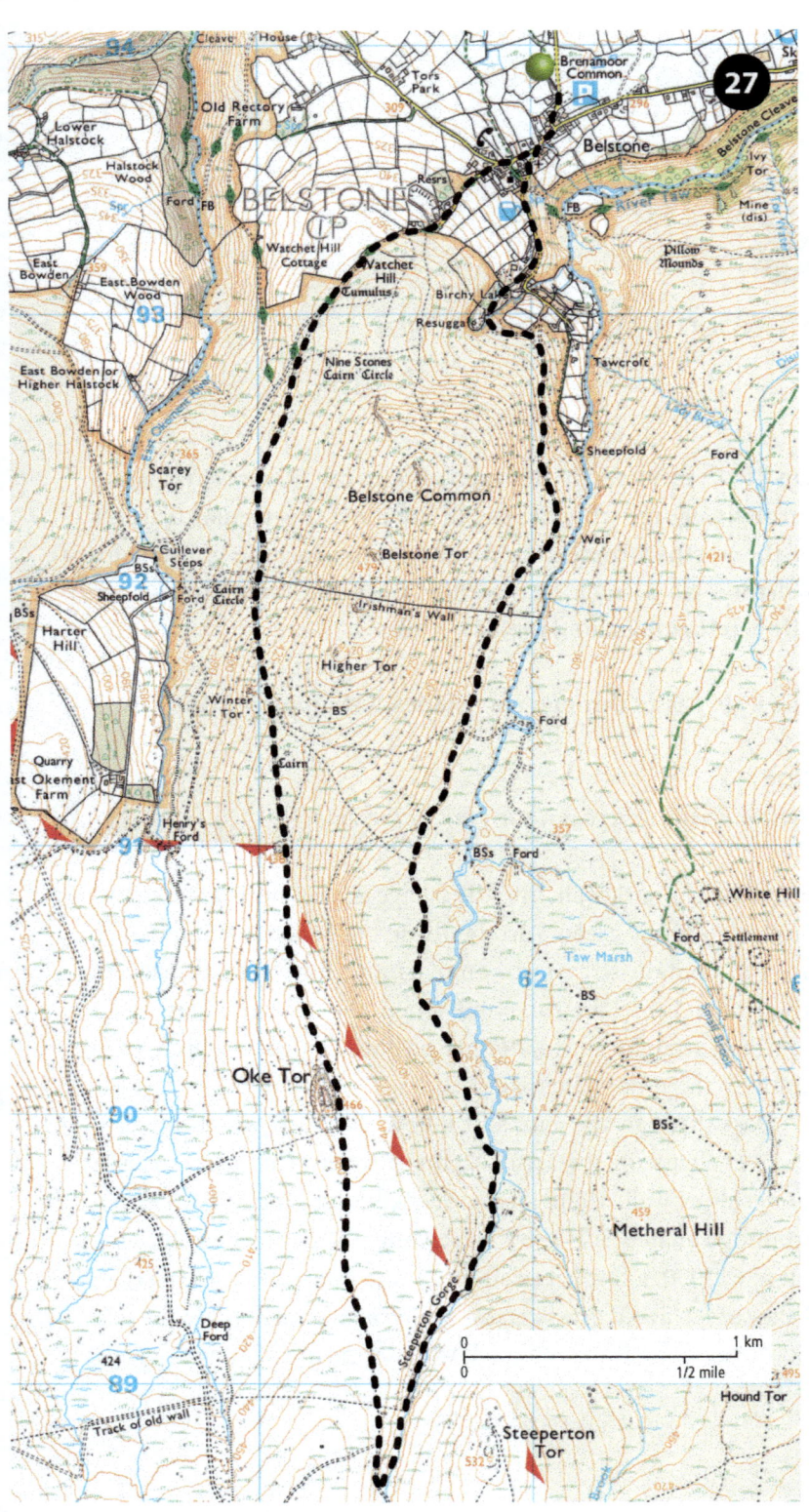

southerly direction for 2 ½ miles to Knack Mine Ford on the River Taw. After a short distance the Nine Maidens stone circle is seen on the left (612928). This is a cairn circle and in fact is made up of considerably more stones than the name suggests. The ridge capped by the Belstone Tors is on the left and the East Okement Valley on the right beyond which are the hills of Northern Dartmoor, including Dartmoor's highest points, High Willhays and Yes Tor.

In about ¾ mile from the stone circle the route is joined by a track from Culliver Steps, right. Here (610920) is an interesting feature known as Irishman's Wall which runs over the ridge to the left, south of Belstone Tor. Crossing (*Guide to Dartmoor*) relates how once an Irishman built this to enclose part of the moor and brought a number of his fellow countrymen to carry out the work. However the local Dartmoor folk objected and met in force to make breaches in the wall which rendered it useless.

Continuing along the track Winter Tor, is passed, right and Higher Tor, left. The track from Culliver Steps soon branches off to the left. Ignore this and continue ahead, noting a mound, left, which contains a cist (611913). The way continues along the ridge with the conical form of Steeperton Tor, with a military hut on the summit, ahead and Taw Marsh below, left beyond which is Cosdon Beacon. The track passes to the left of a grass covered rock known as Knattaborough and then to the left of Oke Tor which also has a military hut. There are a number of tracks beyond Oke Tor, the one to follow leads downhill slightly east of south crossing the route of an old wall, to reach Knack Mine Ford (615885). Ignore another track which branches to the right on the descent.

This is an obvious riverside spot to take a break and refreshment before entering Steeperton Gorge immediately downstream from here. To enter this turn left and follow the left river bank. The path is very narrow and rough in places and for the first couple of hundred yards there is some wet ground and care is needed but it is well worth the effort to see this attractive Dartmoor gem. Keeping quite close to the old wall is the best route to follow.

After emerging from the gorge the route is along Taw Plain, for the most part following the Taw Marsh Waterworks track. However, for the first few hundred yards it is necessary to cross an area of rough ground. There is a narrow path through this which is reached by turning to the left at the bottom of the gorge. If the path is missed, or the ground is too wet for comfort, take a course along the bottom of the hillside, left. A track, which is grassy over the first section, is soon seen which is followed back to Belstone.

Some low-level hatches are noted in the area of Taw Marsh. These are the well-heads of a former SW Water Authority's water extraction plant which was supplied from a large underground lake, the water being piped to Belstone Water Treatment Works. The track soon becomes stony and its course is clear throughout. If desired a short detour to the right may be taken to a ford on the river (620915) which here makes a horseshoe bend; another delightful spot to pause for a while. There is another track near here running parallel with the waterworks track which it joins where the latter crosses the Irishman's Wall (619919).

Continuing towards Belstone the track passes some houses, near the river below right, and on the final section bends left, running uphill for a short distance and then right to the moor gate (618930). From here follow the road to the start, entering Belstone west of the common, beyond which bear right and walk through the village to the car park.

Shovel Down Bronze Age Monuments and Teignhead Farm – 4½ miles

This walk, which for much of its length follows the route of an old peat and farm track known as the Teignhead Road, provides easy access to the upper part of the valley of the North Teign.

Start
North West of Kes Tor, where the road from Chagford, which enters the moor at a cattle grid (667872), turns sharp right to Batworthy. There is parking space here for several cars (662865).

The road, on entering the open moor, passes through an extensive prehistoric settlement with numerous rectangular enclosures and hut circles. A few hundred yards before reaching the car park, on the right, is a prehistoric structure known as Round Pound (663868). It is well worth stopping to view this which consists of two large concentric circular walls. It was excavated by Lady Aileen Fox in the early 1950s which surprisingly showed that iron smelting had been carried out here.

Proceed beyond the car parking space, ascending the bank, and continue along a track which runs parallel to a stone wall, right, to Batworthy Corner (660863), where the wall turns a corner to the right. The track is rather stony in places.

The Shovel Down monuments are on the hillside south from

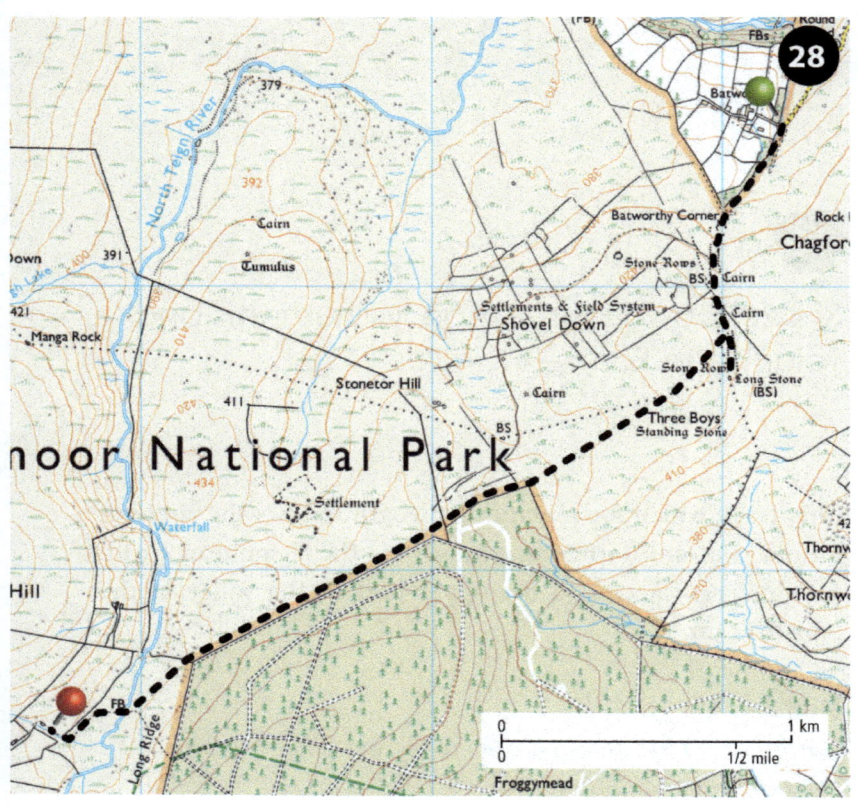

here. To reach these follow a green sunken track south west of south across the moor leading to a point (659860) near the centre of the group just to the left of a fourfold circle. The latter consists of four concentric rings of stones, an unusual feature on Dartmoor. There are five stone rows with traces of a sixth, one single and the others double. These extend in both directions from the fourfold circle and are arranged in a complex manner on an approximately east north east/west south west axis. To the north east of the complex are the remains of a stone circle of which only three stones remain standing.

To the south of the complex is a fine menhir. This is not visible from the fourfold circle but can be reached by following a path which runs left along the stone rows. The menhir is over ten feet high and has been adopted as a boundary stone of the parishes of Lydford, Chagford and Gidleigh. Further south is another stone, the last remaining of a trio known as the Three Boys.

The Teignhead Road, which has been followed from the start of the walk, crossed the stone row by the fourfold circle and took a direct line to the next objective, a corner (653853) of walls above Fernworthy forestry plantations. However it is here only a narrow path over rough ground and a much easier route is to follow another path which crosses the path along the stone rows about half way between the fourfold circle and the menhir. If visiting the menhir it is thus necessary to walk back along the row to reach that crossing point.

The walk then regains the Teignhead Road which continues through a gate and then alongside the wall on the north west side of the plantation. The North Teign valley lies to the right. The track leads on to a stile which is crossed. From here the enclosures and trees associated with the former Teignhead Farm (635844) are seen on the far side of the river below and are easily reached by walking south west downhill across the moor to the Teignhead Clapper. Another branch of the Teignhead Road, which now runs through the Fernworthy plantation, joins the route at the bridge.

Cross the river here and continue, over a tributary the Manga Brook, to the farm enclosures. The farmhouse and associated buildings are now razed to the ground. When I first came here the house was still standing, having been abandoned during the Second World War. It is the setting for Nan Dalton's novel *Tansy's Moor* which gives a graphic account of what life would have been like in the harsh conditions of this remote spot.

On one visit here I witnessed a shepherd driving a flock of sheep across the clapper, a delightful sight. I also met a man here, walking in the direction of Chagford, who said he wanted to get to Buckfast Abbey. I pointed him in the right direction, roughly ninety degrees from the course he had embarked on and told him it would take him two days and to look out for Fox Tor Mire!

This is an interesting spot to spend some time. Below Teignhead Farm, beside the river, are two fine tinners' moulds. There is another clapper a few hundred yards downstream erected in memory of the Dartmoor author the late Harry Starkey. Below this the river runs through the impressive Manga Hole, a gorge with attractive waterfalls. There is a riverside path to this on the left bank running above a stone wall. The Grey Wethers stone circles are about 1 mile south of here, on the slopes of Sittaford Tor.

Return by the same route.

Bibliography

Brewer, Dave, *A Field Guide to the Boundary Markers on and around Dartmoor*
Butler, Jeremy, *Dartmoor Atlas of Antiquities*
Baring-Gould, S *A Book of Dartmoor*
Crossing, William, *Guide to Dartmoor*
Crossing, William, *The Ancient Stone Crosses of Dartmoor*
Conan Doyle, Arthur, *The Hound of the Baskervilles*
Dalton, Nan, *Tansy's Moor*
Dell, Simon and Bright, John, *Dartmoor's Sett Makers, Bankers*
Fleming, Andrew, *The Dartmoor Reaves*
Harrison, Bill, *Dartmoor Stone Crosses*
Hemery, Eric, *The Dartmoor Railroads*
Hemery, Eric, *Walking Dartmoor's Ancient Tracks*
Hemery, Eric, *Walking the Dartmoor Waterways*
Newman, Phil, *The Dartmoor Tin Industry – A Field Guide*
Pettit, Paul, *Prehistoric Dartmoor*
Phillpotts, Eden, *The American Prisoner*
Phillpotts, Eden, *The River*
Robbins, John, *Follow the Leat*
Sandles, Tim, *A Pilgrimage to Dartmoor Crosses*
Stanbrook, Elizabeth, *Dartmoor Forest Farms*
Starkey, F.H., *Dartmoor Crosses & some Ancient Tracks*
Hansford, Worth, R., *Worth's Dartmoor*

APPENDIX 1

Tracks listed by Crossing and Hemery

Track	Walks	Crossing no.	Hemery no.
Tunhill Road	1	51	
Cumston Road	3, 5,	55	26
Sandy Way	3	56	
Lud Gate-Huntingdon	4, 5,	57	
Abbot's Way / Jobber's Road	4, 5, 6	1	3, 4
Owley-Harford	7	62	
Blackwood Path	7	63	6
Monk's Path (Maltern Way)	12, 13	2	12
Black Lane	16	75	2
Postbridge-Dunnabridge Pound	17	80	
Drift Lane	18, 19	78	2
Crockern Farm Track	20, 21	11	
High Down-Amicombe	24	28	
The King Way	24	26	
Okehampton-Dinger Plain	26	34	
Knack Mine Track	27	38	
Birchy Lake-Taw Plain	27	39	
Teignhead Road	28		19

APPENDIX 2

Some other significant paths / tracks incorporated in the walks

Walk	Track
1	Tracks to Top and Pill Tors, Tunhill Rocks and Tunhill Road
2	Wind Tor Car park – Hamel Down
3	Sandy Way – Ryders Hill
4	Huntingdon Warren-Broadafalls
4	Broadafalls-Huntingdon Cross (riverside)
7	Peek Moor Gate-Owley
8	Harford Moor Gate- Piles Copse
10	Scout Hut – Ditsworthy Warren (Edward's Path)
10	Gutter Tor Car park – Ditsworthy Warren
12	Norsworthy Bridge – Down Tor
12	Hingston Hill-Nun's Cross
13	Princetown-Hart Tor
14	Plym Ford – Broad Rock
15, 16	Nun's Cross Ford-Fox Tor
17	Bellever Tor – Laughter Man
19	Postbridge – Waterfall
20	Crocken Farm-Lydford Tor-Lower White Tor
22	Four Winds – Great Mis Tor
25	Meldon – Black Tor
26	Dinger Tor Track to Yes Tor/High Willhays
28	Shovel Down stone rows – Fernworthy plantation corner.